FROM SMUGGLING TO COTTON KINGS

THE GREG STORY

FROM SMUGGLING TO COTTON KINGS

COTTON KINGS

THE GREG STORY

Michael Janes

MEMOIRS

Cirencester

Published by Memoirs

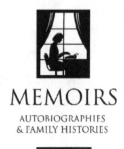

MEMOIRS
AUTOBIOGRAPHIES
& FAMILY HISTORIES

25 Market Place
Cirencester Gloucestershire
GL7 2NX

ISBN 978-0-9565 102-2-8

Printed in England

Contents

	Bibliography	i
	Introduction & acknowledgements	ii
CHAPTER 1	Across the Irish Sea	Page 1
CHAPTER 2	The textile revolution	Page 12
CHAPTER 3	The birth of Quarry Bank	Page 21
CHAPTER 4	Risks and rewards on the high seas	Page 32
CHAPTER 5	The Hibbert connection	Page 37
CHAPTER 6	London banker and country gentleman	Page 43
CHAPTER 7	Aftermath of war	Page 51
CHAPTER 8	Wills and inheritance	Page 60
CHAPTER 9	A new generation	Page 69
CHAPTER 10	Politics and industrial relations	Page 82
CHAPTER 11	Diversification and disposal	Page 94
CHAPTER 12	The Greg heritage	Page 108
	Family Trees	Page 111

Bibliography

1. Robert Philips Greg et al: *Certain Records of the Greg Family 1600-1935*
2. Robert Philips Greg: *Diary of Dates and Recollections 1826-1899*
3. T M Truxes: *Letterbook of Greg & Cunningham 1756-1757*
4. T M Truxes: Defying Empire - *Trading with the Enemy in Colonial New York*
5. Robert Kee: Ireland - *a History*
6. Nini Rodgers: Merchants & Gentlemen - *Lives of Thomas Greg, Waddell Cunningham and William Rainey*
7. Mary B Rose: *The Gregs of Quarry Bank Mill, the Rise and Decline of a Family Firm   1750-1914*
8. Charles F Foster: *Capital and Innovation*
9. T S Ashton: *The Industrial Revolution*
10. P L Cottrell: *Industrial Finance 1830-1914*
11. S D Chapman: *The Cotton Industry in the Industrial Revolution*
12. H McClachlan: *The Unitarian Movement in the Religious Life of England*
13. Sir Thomas Baker: *Memorials of a Dissenting Chapel*
14. Peter Spencer: *Portrait of Samuel Greg 1758-1834*
15. Peter Spencer: *Portrait of Hannah Greg (nee Lightbody) 1766 –1828*
16. Peter Spencer: *Religion at Styal,*
17. London Guildhall Library: *London Directories*
18. L Pressnell: *Country Banking in the Industrial Revolution*
19. John H Clapham: *Economic History of Modern Britain*
20. Frederick Martin: *History of Lloyds & Marine Insurance in Great Britain*
21. Hugh Cockerall: *Lloyds of London*
22. Sheila Ormerod: *The Gregs of Westmill*
23. Guy Ewing: Westmill – *the Story of a Hertfordshire Parish*
24. Jerom Murch: *Memoir of Robert Hibbert, Founder of the Hibbert Trust*
25. Beryl & Allen Freer (Ed): *The Travel Journals of Robert Hyde Greg of Quarry Bank Mill*
26. Walter Wilson Greg: *Biographical Notes 1877-1947*

Introduction and acknowledgments

As a sixth-generation descendant of Thomas Greg of Belfast, I have been fortunate enough to inherit a collection of family records. In later life, I have had time to pursue further researches into the family and this book has been written to describe the Greg family's role in its historical context. Accordingly, the book covers a period when Britain was the cradle of change and innovation in many fields - commerce, agriculture, manufacturing, finance and the development of democratic political structures.

The book goes on to portray the slow decline of a family-based industrial enterprise under the political, social and economic pressures of the late 19th and 20th centuries.

I have had the benefit of access to many published works listed in the bibliography. I am also indebted to the archivists and staff at Quarry Bank Mill and to the Hertfordshire and Norfolk County Councils, The London Guildhall library, Lloyds Insurance Market and others.

I thank my wife Elizabeth for her patient support and other descendants, Kitty Gore, Kath Walker and husband Michael, Sir Richard Lloyd and Andrew Greg for their contributions, help and encouragement.

Michael Janes, MA Oxon, Bsc Econ London

Across the Irish Sea

The Greg family's recorded origins are in Ayrshire, Scotland, and specifically the village of Ochiltree, a few miles south of Kilmarnock, where John Greg, son of James, was born in 1693.

The Gregs later claimed descent from the Macgregors and adopted their crest. Certainly many Greggs, Griegs and Gregs had migrated south to Ayrshire after changing their name after the clan was proscribed by James VI of Scotland. However, the claim sits less comfortably with the family's Presbyterian loyalties. It seems more likely that they were descended from Covenanters, signatories of the 1638 National Covenant that rejected the established church and hierarchy in Scotland.

Ayrshire had been a stronghold of religious free thinkers and a source of migrants to the remote province of Ulster since the early 17th century plantations incentivised Scots and English Calvinists to leave their homes for a country where they would be less of a threat to the established Church. For the first Stuart monarch, James I, head of the Church as well as King, the crown and the Episcopalian church stood or fell together, a perception encapsulated in his expostulation: "No bishop, no king".

In their new home these puritans, mainly Presbyterians, felt secure and began to displace the indigenous Catholic peasantry. A large proportion of early Irish Catholic migrants to North America in the 17th century originated in Ulster.

The Parliamentary victory in the English civil war, the execution of Charles I and the Cromwellian interregnum had brought relief to the Covenanters in Scotland but from 1660 the restored Stuart dynasty began to persecute them, especially James II, who succeeded his brother, Charles

II, in 1685. The so-called bloodless revolution of 1688 dethroned Catholic James in favour of his Protestant daughter Mary and her husband, William of Orange. It also delivered the Covenanters in Scotland from their torment. But with the succession of the obscure German-speaking George I in 1714, they had good reason to fear a reversal of the revolution and the restoration of the Stuarts.

So John Greg sailed for Ulster in 1715 with his new wife Jane and possibly a brother, William, primarily to head off the possibility of renewed persecution in Scotland. It is no coincidence that this was the year of the first Jacobite rebellion, mounted to restore the 'Old Pretender', James Stuart, whose father James II had had Covenanters executed.

John's arrival in Belfast from Ochiltree, aged twenty-one years, is recorded in a Belfast newsletter of the time. The progressive Protestant invasion was having a considerable economic impact on Belfast's rural hinterland. Subsistence farming was giving way to cattle rearing and a thriving livestock trade was developing, with cattle exported from Belfast and other Irish ports.

In Ochiltree, the young John Greg had worked as a blacksmith. It seems he was an enterprising man; in his new home he became a butcher, slaughterman and general provisioner. The focus of his work would have been the preparation of salted beef and pork, for which Ireland was emerging as a preferred supplier for ships' stores, military expeditions and overseas plantations.

Belfast had also become the centre of a booming linen industry, thanks to an influx of French Huguenots skilled in the processing of flax into spun linen yarn. This had increased the demand for better-quality flax from Holland and the Baltic. To these staple items of overseas trade was added a growing demand in northern Europe for more exotic consumer products - notably tea, coffee, sugar, tobacco, wine and port, plus raw materials for construction and fuel, lumber, iron and coal.

Chapter 1

Much of this produce was the result of a century of European colonisation, spearheaded by Dutch, French and British merchant adventurers seeking to replicate the rich pickings of their Spanish predecessors in Mexico and Peru. They set sail for the East Indies, West Indian Islands, Calcutta, America's eastern coastline and Canada, with cargoes of European wares for barter. The risks, both at sea and on land, were considerable and not all of them lived to tell the tale. The pickings from these new territories might not have matched the early Spanish hauls of gold and silver for value, but merchants and planters of sub-tropical produce found a growing market for their new merchandise back home in Europe.

Humbler folk had begun migrating to more temperate lands for the sake of freedom rather than trade or profit, and to practise forms of worship which had been outlawed back home. By the 18th century, dynastic squabbles between European powers had taken on an increasing maritime and colonial dimension as their rulers, stretched for ready cash, saw the opportunity to raise customs revenue. This was carefully nurtured by complex laws to divert trade flows via the mother country.

Irish commerce had been especially damaged by Britain's Navigation Acts of 1685 and 1696, which had closed Irish ports to colonial goods while forcing Irish provisions to the colonies to go via English ports. In 1731, after much lobbying by landowners and merchants, Parliament relaxed the ban on direct shipment of various items, including flaxseed. This gave a much-needed shot in the arm to flax cultivation in Ireland, as well as permitting the direct export of provisions to British colonies.

The change opened up a flourishing trade with North America, especially New York. By the 1740s Belfast had become a busy trading port. It was supported by a prosperous mercantile community, with correspondents in ports in England, northern and southern Europe, the American colonies and the West Indies.

Chapter 1

Business at this time would be done man-to-man, rather than between corporations as it is today. Personal standing and reputation were everything. Mutual trust between individuals and partnerships was crucial to successful trading, especially in maritime trade with its associated long delays in communications. Business links often existed between kinsmen and were reinforced by marriage. Mercantile communities were bound by common interests, shared values and shared forms of worship - in Belfast, typically Presbyterian.

John Greg's business success brought him into the heart of this mercantile fraternity. His sons - John, born in 1716, and Thomas, 1718 - joined him in business at an auspicious time. Thomas exhibited an early talent for business and earned the trust and confidence of important colleagues and correspondents. As his reputation grew he gained access to Irish merchant houses in London, which offered financial services to merchants in the Irish flaxseed trade, accepting their bills of exchange and organising underwriting of cargoes. With good credit and some accumulated capital, he launched his first sea-going vessel, a brig named the Greg, in the early 1740s.

Thomas also had an interest in two other vessels trading with the Baltic and North America. In 1742 he married Elizabeth, daughter of Samuel Hyde, a Lancastrian who had moved to Belfast and become prominent in the linen and provision trades. From the business point of view, this was an excellent match. Though Samuel Hyde died shortly afterwards, Thomas joined his brother-in-law John Hyde in the firm of Leggs, Hyde & Co, Belfast's leading sugar refiners and provisioners.

The direct import of flaxseed was crucial to Thomas' entry into transatlantic trade as it provided dependable winter return cargoes. His ships contributed to the growing export of Irish salted provisions, butter and linen to the West Indies and American mainland, returning with logwood, sugar and other island produce. They would make stops in

Philadelphia, New York and the New England ports to pick up flaxseed and barrel staves. Such reciprocal trade was important not only for freighting economics but for payments, through the two-way availability of trade bills.

Brother John's early career is less well documented, but he too married into a merchant family. He joined a partnership trading with Charleston in South Carolina, where his principle partner, John Torrans, a native of Newry, managed the business. His firm, Torrans, Greg & Pauag, were involved in a number of trades, including slave trafficking.

Greg & Cunningham – a profitable partnership

Waddell Cunningham was born in rural Antrim. Eleven years Thomas' junior, he was working in the linen and flaxseed trade in New York by the 1750s and opened a shop in 1752. As Thomas Greg had done in Belfast, Cunningham ingratiated himself with prominent Irish merchants in New York and was soon able to borrow to fund his trading activities and take part-shares in vessels and flaxseed cargoes bound for Belfast and Newry. Cunningham's business was largely commission trading, which called for little capital but yielded correspondingly modest profits. His ambition was to trade on his own account.

The flaxseed trade soon brought Cunningham into contact with Thomas Greg at Leggs Hyde & Co. Both men felt the need for better control over the quality and marketing of their exports, and each recognised in the other the attributes he valued. Greg admired Cunningham's status in the New York mercantile community, along with his dependability and keen eye for trading opportunities. For his part, Cunningham was impressed by Greg's solid reputation, experience and mercantile connections in the Irish, English and European markets, and particularly by his good credit standing and access to bankers in London.

This was essential for the export of goods to North America, where twelve months' credit was the norm. In May 1756, Greg and Cunningham went into partnership.

Much of New York's maritime trade in the early 1750s, both import and export, contravened Britain's Navigation Acts. These required goods shipped to and from British colonies to be carried in British bottoms and unloaded in British or British colonial ports, with payment of the prescribed duties. Wine shipped from Bordeaux, port from Lisbon, sugar and cotton from the French sugar islands and logwood from Spanish Honduras were technically contraband. So was a wide range of goods from Rotterdam, Hamburg and other Baltic ports, known as the Dutch Trade.

The Treasury in London had avoided too much enforcement of the rules in the decades up to 1750, to avoid hampering the growth of trading activity in America's east coast ports. Such tolerance could be overlooked in peacetime, but there was nothing peaceful about the rivalry between French and English settlers in upstate New York, Pennsylvania and the Ohio valley. In 1754 this dispute broke out into open hostilities, leading to serious reverses for the British militias and some regular forces. This put a different complexion on smuggling activity which "aided the King's enemies" by allowing the shipping of weapons and gunpowder to French forces in Canada.

The formal declaration of war with France in 1756 reignited the naval warfare and privateering in the Atlantic and Caribbean which had characterised earlier conflicts. It also added a new dimension to smuggling, by virtually cutting off France's access to her sugar islands. Deprived of their normal market and source of provisions, these islands were relieved by the merchants of Cork, Belfast, New York, and Philadelphia, who disguised their "aid to the King's enemies" by diverse subterfuges. They would ship disproportionately large volumes to neutral ports such as Spanish Monte Cristo on San Domingo, or small Dutch and

Danish colonies, for onward shipment to the French islands. They would suborn customs officials to provide false shipping documents, fit out privateers and, when challenged by British naval ships, pass off cargoes of French produce as lawful prizes of war. They would also carry French prisoners, so that if they were apprehended in French waters they could offer them in exchange for British captives under lawful arrangements agreed between the combatant powers.

A new British-appointed Governor of New York, arriving in 1755, had some success in closing down the 'Dutch trade' before the formal outbreak of war. But for the town's merchant community, that would be compensated by the contraband from the French sugar islands and the prize money from privateering against French merchant shipping. Enforcement of the law was impeded by corrupt and venal customs officials, sympathetic Assemblymen and less-than-staunch members of the Province of New York's judiciary, some of them relatives or associates of the law breakers. Irish merchants were especially prominent in the illegal traffic and Waddell Cunningham emerged as one of the most brazen, facing several prosecutions.

The Seven Years War with France would bear out Cunningham's confident predictions and prove extremely profitable to Thomas Greg, not only through the New York partnership but also through Leggs Hyde & Co, who shipped Irish provisions and linen to the French Islands direct from Belfast. Although fines had been imposed and some contraband cargoes seized, the losses were small relative to the high wartime profit margins, not only on smuggled cargoes but also on prize cargoes of French West Indian produce landed in New York. In addition Greg and Cunningham had an interest, in terms of prize money yielded, in one of the most successful privateers in the Atlantic.

Chapter 1

Patronage and business in Ireland

Thomas Greg's war profits enabled him to buy land close to Belfast and obtain long leases from the Earl of Donegal on extensive land in northern Ulster. He was also able to finance the construction of a canal linking Belfast with Lisburn, centre of the Irish linen industry. Waddell Cunningham likewise emerged a wealthy man, and in 1762 he led the speculative purchase of a portion of the Hardenberg Patent land in the Catskill Mountains in upstate New York. Greg took a half share in this.

The end of the war the following year, however, brought a sharp contraction in the New York partnership's trade, which was left to be managed by junior partners following Cunningham's departure under a cloud in 1764. Convicted of an assault on another merchant, he had unwisely appealed judgement to the British Privy Council, which incurred the wrath of a New York trading community enraged by the British Treasury's efforts to raise colonial taxes to pay for the war - a foretaste of the later revolution and War of Independence.

After a spell in London, Cunningham returned to Belfast in 1765, forming a separate partnership with Thomas Greg and his eldest son, another John, under the name of Gregs and Waddell Cunningham of Belfast, a partnership cemented by Cunningham's marriage to Thomas' sister-in-law, Margaret Hyde.

While provisioning continued a staple activity, the post-war focus of Thomas' business switched to trade within the British Isles, and manufacturing centred on Lisburn. In September 1763 he and his wife were reported as entertaining a crowd of "upwards of 1000" with a band and refreshments to celebrate the first voyage of his 60-ton lighter the Lord Hertford, laden with coal and timber, up to Lisburn.

In 1765, Thomas opened a shop in the town. The next year he and Cunningham set up a plant to make vitriol for bleaching linen fibres on an island in the Lagan river at Lisburn. In 1769 Thomas embarked on the construction of the Chichester quay on the Farset river, to accommodate more vessels of larger draft. Financing these investments called for some borrowing on mortgage.

The Belfast Gregs' Presbyterian allegiance took second place to their social and business advancement, and they were at pains to court Ulster's landed aristocracy, especially the Chichester family, Earls of Donegal and the absentee landowners of most of Belfast. Beside the Chichester quay, Thomas Greg named his newly-built vessel, launched in 1765, the Countess of Donegal. In the 1770s both Thomas Greg and Waddell Cunningham leased land from the Earl. Cunningham also acted as his steward and was involved in disputes and tenant evictions over increased rents.

Thomas Greg and his brother also gained the favour of Wills Hill, Earl of Hillsborough and later first Marquess of Downshire. Hillsborough strode the corridors of power at Westminster, figuring in several short-lived Cabinets in the 1760s and 1770s. He became a proponent of the later incorporation of Ireland into the union of England and Scotland under a single Parliament in London.

Hillsborough must have felt indebted to the brothers in some way. As Colonial Secretary, he appointed John Greg Secretary to the Commissioners for the sale of lands in islands ceded by France under the 1763 Treaty of Paris which ended the war. No doubt John's experience of plantations in his Irish trading partnership helped to earn him this post.

John Greg spent some time in the West Indies organising auctions of former French plantations. His inside knowledge enabled him to bid successfully for one of the more cultivable plantation sites with sea access in the otherwise mountainous terrain of Dominica, renaming it the Hillsborough Estate after his patron. In 1773 his wife Catherine inherited a smaller plantation, Cane Garden, on the island of St Vincent. Over the next seventy years three Gregs would successively be slave owners, though none of them visited their plantations. Later the Earl helped Thomas to secure exclusive rights to royal minerals in Antrim, Derry and Down.

Between 1743 and 1764 Elizabeth Greg bore Thomas thirteen children. Some died in infancy or early childhood. The first to reach adulthood was John, born in 1746. He became a partner in Gregs and Cunningham in Belfast and was despatched to manage their joint interests in New York State, but he died around 1780, still in his mid thirties.

The family's subsequent history revolves around the main survivors. Sisters Mary and Jane were born in 1748 and 1750 respectively. They were followed by Thomas, Samuel and Cunningham, born in 1752, 1758 and 1762, and finally Eleanor, born in 1759. This was a large family, as is clear from a portrait of the early 1760s.

By contrast, brother John had no children. Nor did Waddell Cunningham. Launching the male progeny into rewarding careers became an increasing preoccupation for Thomas - a story which is covered in the next chapter.

The early 1770s brought a contraction in credit. These were difficult times for John Greg senior, still a prominent figure in Belfast's provisioning trade, whose business failed. The collapse affected the sons' business standing and their two partnerships were dissolved to protect the assets of partners Waddell Cunningham and John Hyde. Fortunately, with the sale of father John's Belfast properties in Belfast in 1774, stability returned. The partnership between Thomas and John Greg re-established its position as suppliers of imported products from its shops in Belfast and Lisburn and as producers of salt beef from Thomas' extensive grazing pastures.

But by the late 1780s Thomas' fortunes were also declining. He explored unsuccessfully for coal, and lost money from a china and glass company which he had founded at Ballymacerat. When offered a baronetcy by the Earl of Hillsborough he was advised by his son Thomas that he did not have the means to support the title.

Chapter 1

In later life John Greg took up residence in Hampton, south of London, where he died in 1795. Thomas died the following year, his reputation high, thanks to the benefits he had brought to Belfast's trade and industry.

The impact of the brothers' wills on the generation that followed is covered in the chapters that follow.

The textile revolution

We know that by the 1770s the business climate in Ulster was looking less rosy than it had in earlier decades. Thomas and Elizabeth Greg had a large brood and Thomas must have been much troubled by the challenge of securing profitable careers for his sons.

Perhaps this is why, in 1768, he sent two of them off to seek their fortunes elsewhere. Ten-year old Samuel Greg and his sixteen-year-old brother Thomas were told to say their goodbyes to Belfast and their family and put on a ship for England.

The boys were not truly emigrating. Ireland still had its own Parliament in Dublin, but was subject to the English Crown, represented by a Lord Lieutenant and substantially controlled by the government in Westminster through the Irish Secretary.

Trading links with England were strong and growing. Besides cattle and agricultural produce, Ireland was supplying materials for textiles, flax and locally-spun linen yarns which were in demand for cloth manufacture and imported English dry goods, cloth, tools and machinery.

In England as in Ulster, kinship was a crucial factor for success in business. The boys' mother's family, the Hydes, had been in commerce on both sides of the Irish Sea since Samuel Hyde, Thomas' father-in-law, had migrated from Lancashire to Belfast some decades before. But crucially his second son Robert Hyde had remained in England, going into partnership in Manchester with Robert Hamilton to manufacture linen and fustian, a thick twilled short-napped cotton cloth.

The businesses on the two sides of the water were to an extent complementary, as Hyde and Hamilton's Belfast relatives were among their suppliers. Hamilton had been working in the linen business for many years and had particular experience of the American market, having been in a partnership in New York up to 1754. He brought to the table a keen awareness of colonial fashions, which enabled the firm to develop patterns to suit the New World market.

The two Roberts would visit New York from time to time to maintain their contacts, but otherwise they relied on Greg and Cunningham to represent them and act as purchasing agents for raw cotton, the fibre used for weft thread for weaving with linen warps into fustian. Just to be clear on these terms, the warp was a spread of multiple threads attached to the loom. They were under greater tension than the weft thread inserted by the shuttle between alternate warp threads to create a woven fabric.

In 1762 the Hyde and Hamilton partnership was dissolved and Robert Hyde took his brother Nathaniel on as partner.

The families who have featured in this story so far all had something else in common apart from their trades - they were dissenters, Christians who rejected the established church, the Church of England, with its bishops and liturgy. Though sectarian animosities had relaxed considerably since the 1688 revolution, the activities of dissenters were still restricted by laws from the Restoration era barring them from holding Crown or municipal office, from standing for Parliament or holding commissions in the army or navy. They were even excluded from the Oxford and Cambridge colleges.

While in one sense second-class citizens, wealthy dissenting families in centres like Manchester, Liverpool, Leeds, Belfast and Birmingham formed their own mini-aristocracies. Their status and achievements drew increasing recognition from the landed classes which still pulled the political levers.

Understandably, the dissenters retained a clannish instinct to protect for posterity the wealth their enterprise and industry had accumulated.

Family obligations were particularly powerful. Fathers regarded it as their clear duty to find business openings for their sons and advantageous marriages for their daughters. Brothers took responsibility for unmarried sisters, and uncles for nephews.

Robert Hyde faced the opposite dilemma to his brother-in-law. Where Greg had a large brood to launch into adult life, Hyde no direct male descendant and his brother Nathaniel had produced seven daughters but no sons.

No doubt this is why he offered to adopt Samuel, aptly named after his maternal grandfather. Where Thomas, the older brother, stood in this arrangement is not clear. However we do know the brothers left for England together, never to return except for occasional social visits.

From cottage industry to 'satanic' mills

The focus of the story now moves to the early career of young Samuel Greg. On his arrival in England, he was sent to school in York and then to Harrow, where he was taught by a Dr Parr, "a noted Greek scholar and flogger" according to Samuel's son Robert. From there he recorded: "Robert Hyde, born 1723, intended to bring up my father to his own business but, Nathaniel Hyde being jealous, Robert Hyde proposed to send him to India and afterwards buy for him the rectory of Prestwich and make a parson of him. This, however, not suiting my father's views or tastes, he was put to the business in Chancery Lane....... My father when au fait travelled for two years on the Continent, taking orders for the House of Hyde, and becoming a regular manufacturer of all Manchester stuffs, chiefly velveteens, nankeens, quiltings &c .... Robert Hyde made my father partner, gave him £10,000 and, when he died in 1782, left him heir to all his property, in case Nathaniel should have no sons who should arrive at the age of twenty-one".

Chapter 2

The term "manufacturer" did not at this time carry the modern connotation of a factory-based process. It simply meant the production of woven cloth or piece goods. In the 1770s the processes of preparing, spinning and weaving textile fibres were still largely done in private homes - the original 'cottage industry'. The manufacturer's role was that of organising and financing the separate stages, procuring the raw wool, linen or cotton, then delivering it to the cottagers to be combed or carded by hand or spun on the wheel. Some of it was sent to be wound and treated into sized warps for weaving or hanks for knitting.

Woven cloth production typically involved whole families, with women and children carding, combing and spinning weft cotton and the male weaver being paid per yard of cloth produced for collection and shipment to the manufacturer's warehouse. It was called the "putting-out system", and for the manufacturer it involved little fixed capital apart from the warehouse itself - the looms were usually the weaver's property - but substantial working capital was needed to hold stocks at all stages and allow for the extended credit expected by customers.

Fustian was the Hyde brothers' principal product. It is first recorded in the 14th century as a coarse cloth made from diverse raw materials, but primarily wool and linen derived from flax. As trade with the Near East expanded, cotton also appeared as a weft thread, which improved its ability to take up dyes.

The emergence of the British and Dutch East India Companies in 1600 and 1602 triggered the import of a new fabric - 100% cotton calicos and chintzes. Craftsmen in several Indian centres succeeded in dyeing and printing these in colours that were much brighter than anything produced in Europe. They were also fast to sunlight and repeated washing.

As time went on, the merchant companies could specify increasingly complex designs to suit changing European tastes. With the growth of prosperity in the 17th century the new fabrics became a "must have" among the European upper classes, for both clothing and soft furnishings. Meanwhile plain grey cloth, imported undyed, stimulated the growth of dyeing and block printing in Europe. In England this industry was at first concentrated in London.

Though raw cotton had long been imported into Europe to be spun on the wheel and used by stocking-frame knitters and as weft for handloom weavers, it would not be successfully used as a warp thread for weaving until the 1780s. Governments were pressed by manufacturing interests to introduce protective measures against the imported cotton goods. Parliament duly prohibited the use of Indian chintzes in 1701 and imposed an import duty on printed linen and calico in 1712, doubling it two years later. Then in 1721 the use and wear of all printed or dyed calicos was prohibited. Though the ban was repealed in 1774, the import duties stayed until 1831 and were progressively increased.

The key feature of fustian woven from a linen warp and a cotton weft was its classification as linen rather than calico in the legislation. This gave it a preference in the home market against imported calicos, to offset calico's superior performance for dyeing and printing. Besides expanding the market for fustian and the demand for linen and cotton yarn centred in Manchester, the rules encouraged the growth of local dyeing and printing, an activity which progressively migrated from London to Lancashire. Here printers proved especially innovative, developing printing by copper plates and then cylinders, a process perfected by the Peels of Blackburn.

Preparing linen warps for weaving was itself a labour-intensive multi-stage process. First the flax had to be harvested and dried, then heckled. This was a manual process to sort out the fibres by length for onward movement to spinners, many of them smallholders who worked only part-time. The spun yarn was then bleached and wound on to warps by other specialists, for delivery to the handloom weavers in their cottages.

Chapter 2

The demand for sailcloth, both for merchant shipping and naval vessels, had been a driving force behind linen manufacture. The growth of the fustian market now put additional pressure on the resources for growing, processing and spinning flax. The quality of the flax was especially important - the best flax was imported from the Baltic. The lengthy time cycle from raw material to finished cloth required a heavy outlay of working capital. All this contributed to the pressure to match the 100% imported cotton product. Such was the commercial and technical background to Samuel Greg's entry into the cloth industry in Manchester.

Robert Greg's account of his father's early career shows how the success of a business revolved around families, and particularly the ability of their male members. Nathaniel Hyde, Samuel's uncle, was some 18 years younger than Robert Hyde and a drunkard and gambler. What a contrast with Samuel this must have seemed to the older brother.

Nevertheless Robert was careful not to disinherit any son that might yet be born to his brother. In the event, Nathaniel's wife delivered a son after his death in 1797. Samuel became the boy's guardian until he was old enough to inherit.

However, Nathaniel had retired straight after his brother's death in 1782 and, to clear his debts, had sold his share in the warehouse stocks to the remaining partners, John Middleton and Samuel Greg. The valuation was depressed by the war with the American colonies, but the peace that followed gave it a huge uplift, yielding Samuel Greg a windfall profit of £14,000.

It would be difficult to overstate the importance to Samuel's subsequent career of the inheritance he received from the Hydes. Even more important than the money was the training in management, finance and marketing in a large and complex business, while the Hydes' connections with other families among the dissenting business community in Manchester and Liverpool gave him enhanced access to trade credit.

Chapter 2

This, with the Hydes' experience, made him especially aware of the mismatch between the growing capacity of handloom weavers, increased by the introduction of the fly shuttle, and the limited volumes of cotton yarns that could be produced on the domestic spinning wheel. The output of the latter had been helped by the spinning jenny, which enabled the spinner to operate several spindles at once, but its inventor, Samuel Hargreaves, had been hounded out of Lancashire in 1768 by cottage spinners fearing loss of employment. Meanwhile Jedediah Strutt's improvement to the stocking frame was increasing the output of the Nottingham and Derby knitters to meet the demand for cheaper cotton hosiery. But production was constrained by shortage of spun yarn, so Hargreaves and his invention found a ready refuge in Nottingham.

Meanwhile the pressure was on the Manchester woven-cloth manufacturers to expand cotton yarn production for weft in the loom. The jenny was not patented, and the Lancashire firms developed machines which could be operated by women and children, with up to eighty spindles.

Nevertheless, jenny spinning remained a largely domestic operation. William Radcliffe of Stockport noted that out of fifty or sixty local farmers, only six or seven were covering their costs from farm produce. "The rest got their rent partly in some branch of trade such as spinning and weaving woollen, linen or cotton. The cottagers were employed entirely in this manner except for a few weeks in the harvest" wrote Radcliffe.

He went on to record how in the 1770s and 1780s the burgeoning demand for cheap calicos had transformed local spinning: "That of wool disappeared altogether and that of linen was also nearly gone - cotton, cotton, cotton, was almost the universal material of employment .... the yarn was all spun on the jenny". It is clear that in Stockport by 1789 jenny yarn was being produced up to very fine counts for weaving muslin.

If one invention can be given the credit for the birth of the factory system in England it was the water frame, developed by former barber and wig-maker Richard Arkwright. This was a heavier piece of kit than the human arm could drive. Arkwright initially tried to address this problem with horse power before turning to water power supplied by fast-flowing streams, on the model of flour milling.

In 1771 Arkwright established his first mill at Cromford in Derbyshire, driven by the flow of the River Derwent. The water frame greatly increased the spinner's output. By drawing out the fibres between fluted rollers geared to turn at different speeds, it also produced a more regular and stronger cotton yarn that could withstand the tension of the stocking frame and, suitably dressed, serve as a warp thread in the loom. This technical superiority made it a crucial breakthrough in the manufacture of cotton hosiery and home-produced woven calicos and chintzes.

Alone among the early developers of spinning machinery, Arkwright obtained patents from Parliament. In 1769 he secured one for spinning with rollers, and in 1775 one for carding with cylinders. The latter was widely infringed by manufacturers, who assembled groups of jenny spinners around a single unlicensed engine. Arkwright tried to enforce the 1775 patent at court, but a key 1781 Court of King's Bench judgement upheld the objections of the Manchester manufacturers.

The patents were by no means the most formidable hurdles to the adoption of the new water-powered technology. Manufacturers also had to find suitable sites on watercourses and fund the heavy and risky fixed investment needed for buildings, machinery and dams. They needed to secure the supply of sufficient quantity and quality of raw cotton and recruit labour from the thinly-populated rural neighbourhoods where the necessary water power could be found.

By the early 1780s Samuel Greg was under great pressure to take advantage of the expiry of the patents. He was much frustrated by the weaknesses of the putting-out system, the diseconomies of moving multiple small volumes of raw materials and woven cloth to and from the cottage-based producers, and the lack of control over the quality of the product and the workflow. To alleviate these problems the Hydes had set up a weaving shed at Eyam in Derbyshire. Its output, however, was severely restricted by the shortage of cotton yarn.

Like many others in Lancashire at the time, Samuel Greg saw the answer to the constraints on his cloth business in a water-powered mill on the Arkwright model. Fortunately, he had the resources to invest in his vision on a larger scale than most of his competitors.

Chapter 3

The birth of Quarry Bank

Samuel Greg had a deeper purse than most other aspiring mill owners and enjoyed a good credit rating following the post-war boom in the Manchester cloth trade. He simply needed to find the right site for his new venture, and choose a partner with the experience to make up for his own lack of technical knowledge.

Samuel found the site he wanted at Quarry Bank, in the valley of the fast-moving River Bollin at Styal, Cheshire. In 1783, having leased the land from the Earl of Stamford, he set about building his mill.

His first partner, John Massey, died before the mill started up, to be replaced by Matthew Fawkner, who remained in place for the next twelve years. During this period Samuel remained, like many others, an absentee mill owner, living at 85 King Street, Manchester, a property he had inherited from his uncle which enabled him to continue supervising his cloth business in Chancery Lane nearby. As late as 1791 he was still described in the list of members of the Manchester Literary and Philosophical Society as "fustian manufacturer of King Street, Manchester".

The first mill at Quarry Bank cost about £3,000 to build and equip, a modest sum in relation to the total business. A pioneering census of Arkwright-type mills in England, Scotland and Wales in 1788 listed it among 143 of its type. Later studies suggested this had been as an underestimate, but in fact most of these early mills were small converted corn mills or even cottages.

Quarry Bank's original capacity was chiefly absorbed in supplying coarse yarns to Eyam. There were diverse problems in the early years, such as the uneven quality of raw cotton from various sources and the inadequacy of the first water wheel, which was replaced in 1792.

Labour was another constraint. Men who were comfortable with factory life were scarce and difficult to recruit, so the mill owners turned to women and children. There were many menial tasks for children in the mills, and they could be trained up to the more skilled operations.

In the late 18th century, mill owners in rural neighbourhoods found apprentices between ten and twelve years old easy to recruit from poorhouses in the towns, where they were a burden on the poor rate, or by agreement with poor families. In the more remote locations it was more economic to build an 'apprentice house' for the youngsters rather than cottages, as required by adult workers and their families. The first apprentices at Quarry Bank were lodged with local families, but by 1790 there were enough to support an apprentice house, which was built together with some cottages for adult workers. By 1800 parish apprentices made up around half the total workforce of just under 200. Other mill owners had more.

Social historians have justifiably dwelt on the exploitation of child labour in the early cotton mills, the long hours, the dangerous working conditions and the general neglect. It should be remembered however that working long hours, either in the home, the farm or the cottage smallholding, was the standard lot of children in those days. In many ways Quarry Bank must have been typical of the 'dark satanic mills' disdained by William Blake, but it was certainly not among the worst. By the standards of the times Samuel Greg took his obligations to his young employees seriously and was conscientious about feeding, clothing, housing and supporting them. Some children inevitably truanted, but the records show they were driven by the desire to see their families rather than the need to escape their working conditions.

Chapter 3

An advantageous marriage

It is appropriate at this point to revert again to the sectarian issues which were still very much alive in Britain at the turn of the 18th century. Historians have noted the high incidence of Unitarians among the entrepreneurs of the Industrial Revolution. It is worth tracing the emergence of this sect within the post-Restoration non-conformity, and its impact on society.

Rejection of the Trinity was seen as a heresy in the reformed churches, as in the Roman church. However controversy within English Protestant circles in the 17th century had focused as much on the issues of church government as theology, mirroring the constitutional issue between king and Parliament that troubled the early Stuart kings. The abolition of bishops with the prayer book were early steps taken by the Presbyterian-dominated Parliament of 1640, reluctantly summoned by an impecunious Charles I to vote him taxes.

Their reinstatement was one of the first acts of the Royalist pro-Anglican Parliament summoned by the restored Charles II. But in the interim, English Church government had been remodelled on Presbyterian lines, with countywide Presbyteries divided into groups or classes of parishes. For many Puritans even that had been unacceptably authoritarian and hierarchical, and some congregations had broken away to become self-governing, under the name of Independents. The more orthodox retained the Presbyterian label, but the class structure fell into decay.

In the decades that followed, the various non-conformist congregations and ministers remained determined to maintain their forms of worship in the face of the new laws. With no tithe income and little endowment, they depended on the financial support of their members to provide even modest stipends to their ministers.

Chapter 3

Training for the ministry presented another problem. How could one prepare Presbyterian or Independent recruits when the necessary instruction in classics and theology was in the hands of the grammar schools and Anglican-run universities?

So the ministers, under pressure to earn additional income, offered to tutor fee-paying pupils as boarders in their own homes, a practice that led to the establishment of the so called academies - a title that belied the small number of pupils involved. Though they took on the names of the towns and communities they served, these academies depended crucially on their leading tutors, who might be removed at any moment to a chapel in some far-off town. Consequently, many did not last very long.

Nonetheless the academies played their part in the education of an expanding urban middle class. In contrast to the comfortable torpor which characterised the well-endowed Anglican Church and the old universities of the 18th century, the non-conformist circles associated with the academies fostered a spirit of intellectual enquiry, criticism and innovation. The tutors were increasingly of the Unitarian persuasion, and were eloquent in propagating it. Some were men of high intellect whose interests in the Age of Enlightenment extended beyond classics and theology into mathematics and the natural sciences.

The free-thinking theologian and chemist Joseph Priestley was a celebrated example. Priestley, who isolated and identified the element oxygen, was a friend of the industrialists Josiah Wedgewood, Matthew Boulton and James Watt. The broader curricula of academies such as Warrington - where Priestley taught in the 1760s - and their acceptance of pupils of all persuasions attracted a wider field of students. Some of them were bent on business careers and enrolled to escape from the narrow focus of the grammar schools, with their emphasis on Latin texts and Anglican theology. The spirit of empirical enquiry nurtured by the academies would help to feed the technical advances of the industrial revolution.

Chapter 3

As one of the mercantile families of Manchester, the Hydes savoured the new thinking. The Chapel they attended in Cross Street, established by Presbyterians in the 1690s, flourished during the 18th century under the leadership of trustees who were ready to encourage new interpretations of the scriptures and choose free-thinking ministers, men who were soon openly preaching Unitarian doctrine.

Samuel Greg, as the Hydes' adopted nephew, may have gained some intellectual stimulus from Unitarian society, but more importantly he secured business connections, as the Chapel was dominated by tradespeople. A published history of the Chapel of 1884 shows that by the mid 18th century most of the listed trustees were linen drapers or merchants, with the odd manufacturer or banker as time went on.

Unitarianism was equally strong in the merchant circles of Liverpool, where the Hydes negotiated their cotton supply through the house of Rathbone. It was this connection that introduced Samuel to Hannah Lightbody, youngest of three daughters and heiresses of the late Adam Lightbody, a wealthy Unitarian linen merchant. Before their marriages the girls had attracted the nickname of "the heavy Misses Lightbodies". The couple were married in late 1789.

No doubt Samuel was pleased with his £10,000 marriage settlement. Young Hannah however, must have met something of a challenge on joining her new husband's household at King Street - she had to share her home with an unmarried sister-in-law, and sometimes two of them.

Hannah traced her descent through her mother's side to the Oxford-educated divine Philip Henry, whose Calvinist principles forbade his signing the 1662 Act of Uniformity as conflicting with the ordination vows he had made in Cromwell's time. Henry's principles lost him his living and prevented him from preaching within five miles of incorporated towns. He even saw the inside of a prison on more than one occasion. His son Matthew would prove a still more radical free thinker in questioning the accepted interpretations of the scriptures.

Chapter 3

Unitarianism was a powerful force in Hannah's upbringing and among the circle of Liverpool intelligentsia she frequented. Her education included several years as a parlour boarder at a Unitarian school in Stoke Newington, London, a noted hotbed of dissent. But she was never an intolerant sectarian. In fact Unitarianism bred in her above all a powerful conviction of the benefits of learning and a cultured society.

The comings and goings of merchants and traders preoccupied with money-making, along with a series of pregnancies, must have made life at 85 King Street irksome and stressful for Hannah. Her letters poignantly express her longing for the society she had known in Liverpool, and she did her best to cultivate similar society in Manchester. Samuel, who did not share his wife's strong intellectual mindset, was nonetheless persuaded to join the Manchester Literary and Philosophical Society, and its members would adjourn to King Street after meetings.

By the standards of his time Samuel was a sensitive husband, able to appreciate his wife's qualities. It was primarily to relieve her unhappiness that he rented Oak Farm, close to the new mill at Styal, as a summer residence for her and their children.

1789 saw the outbreak of the French Revolution, followed three years later by the overthrow of the mighty French monarchy and the execution of the royal family. These cataclysmic events set off reverberations throughout Europe, which alarmed the ruling classes. But it was the impact on Ireland that most concerned the Gregs. The radical Protestant Wolfe Tone had already attracted support among Belfast Presbyterians for his Society of United Irishman, which aimed to unite Catholics with dissenters, both victims of new penal laws that reinforced the dominance of the Anglican Church and the privileges of its adherents.

In Belfast old Thomas Greg, now well into his seventies and still dependent on the favour of aristocratic landlords, was desperate to steer clear of politics and acutely embarrassed by the sympathies some of his adult offspring showed for the radicals. These tensions increased sharply after hostilities broke out between France and England in 1793. Wolfe Tone fled to Paris to persuade the revolutionary government that Ireland, ripe for rebellion, was the weak link in England's defences. In 1796 a French expedition to Bantry Bay was defeated only by the weather. A second expedition with Tone himself on board led to an insurrection of Catholic peasantry in Wicklow. It was put down with much bloodshed in 1798. Tone was executed and the Society, with its clandestine cells of Defenders, suppressed.

Presbyterians in Belfast had been implicated in the United Ireland movement, and suspicion fell on the Gregs there. In 1797 the home of Samuel's younger brother, Cunningham, was partly sacked by General Lake's soldiers. Jane Greg, the older unmarried sister, who had voiced her sympathies for the Irish republican cause, was forced to leave town and seek asylum with Samuel in England. Samuel's daughter, Ellen Melly, later wrote that her mother had "feared domiciliary visits; for my father was the only Irishman in the town and his sister Jane had been obliged to leave Ireland".

It seems Jane Greg never returned to Ireland. She died in 1817 and is buried with Hannah and Samuel in the family vault at Wilmslow Parish Church.

Back in England the boom in piece goods of the mid-1780s did not last. Samuel's venture in the American market with his Irish partner, his brother-in-law James Lyle, produced little apart from bad debts. But the war was changing markets, and a new demand emerged for the better quality cotton warp yarns produced by the water frame. Against this background, Samuel's business focus changed. from cloth trading in Manchester to expanding yarn production at Quarry Bank well beyond the requirement at Eyam.

In 1796 he had formed a new partnership with Peter Ewart, previously an engineer at the Soho factory of steam engine makers Boulton & Watt, who sent him north to sell steam engines to the spinning mills. The two men set about expanding their spinning capacity. The water power was raised by a dam and weir, and by 1800 two new wheels had been added. More workers were taken on, both children and adults, and new cottages built.

In the same year the Gregs began the construction of a new home next to Quarry Bank Mill. Though it was conceived primarily as a holiday refuge for Hannah and her growing family, Quarry Bank House also matched the changing focus of Samuel's business. As the family gravitated more and more towards their new home, Hannah Greg had an increasing influence over the mill's operation, especially the care and upbringing of the child apprentices. Samuel came to rely on her judgement on many issues affecting the recruitment and care of both juvenile and adult labour, including their spiritual needs.

The Health and Morals of Apprentices Act 1802 required the mill owner to provide for children's religious instruction and a new clause was duly introduced in the Quarry Bank indentures. Although restrictions on non-conformity had been relaxed, there was no dissenting chapel in the neighbourhood. Samuel, who knew the Rector of St Bartholomew's in Wilmslow as signatory of his indentures, arranged for his apprentices to attend two services each Sunday to fulfil this new obligation, paying for instance £3.15s for 3 years "pew rent" in 1814. Hannah and her children also attended St Bart's, though an 1820 diary entry by her unmarried daughter Marianne recorded: "At this time the church was deserted, few attended except ourselves and the apprentices. Mr Dixon, the curate, was an indifferent preacher and there was no rector, two different ones having been appointed by Mr Trafford and the Crown". This is an example of contemporary Anglican malpractice.

The decline of St Barts continued, while efforts by Congregationalists and Methodists to attract the villagers made insufficient headway. It seems to have contributed to Hannah's concern for the morals of the growing adult population. With daughters Marianne and Hannah behind her, she persuaded Samuel to finance the construction of a chapel. The Oak Chapel, later renamed Norcliffe Chapel by Samuel's son Robert, was built in 1822. There was some dispute over the choice between visiting Methodist lay preachers favoured by the millworkers and a permanent pastor, the solution preferred by the Gregs. In the event, after a Congregationalist and a Baptist had both managed to upset the family, their confidence was won by a Unitarian, though his sermons were said to be too difficult for most of the congregation to understand.

Meanwhile during the Napoleonic wars, which continued from 1793-1815 with a brief interval at the turn of the century, cotton spinning had expanded rapidly, spurred by rising profits. As technology advanced, it had also changed. While the mills of the 1780s had been built to supply manufacturers and knitters with their own yarn needs, the success of the new processes and the rapid growth in demand had generated an active market in yarns as an end product. In 1807 the Eyam weaving shed closed, a victim of high yarn prices and a shortage of weavers.

While some larger rural mills on fast streams had been expanded - those of the Arkwrights, Strutts and Robert Owen at New Lanark being larger than Quarry Bank - dependence on water power was being relieved by harnessing steam power. This was either to supplement water power or to drive new mills in towns free of the labour constraints of the countryside, a persistent problem in rural mills.

At the same time the 'mule' developed by Samuel Crompton back in 1779 had combined the twisting action of the jenny with the regularising capability of the water frame. Free of patent protection, it now became the preferred technology for both water and steam-powered mills. Arkwright's water frame could not match the mule's capability of spinning up to 80s counts (80 hanks of 840 yards per pound of yarn). In addition to fine calicos, mule yarns enabled Samuel Oldknow at Mellor to produce muslins, hitherto virtually the monopoly of skilled Swiss artisans.

Chapter 3

The partnership with Peter Ewart proved a fruitful match: Ewart's engineering knowhow with Greg's capital. Under the partnership agreement Ewart contributed only £400 in capital, but took a quarter of the profits from spinning and a sixth of those from marketing, while Greg financed the investment outlay on which the partnership paid an annual rent.

Ewart was keen to invest the partnership's profits in the new technology. After installing a steam engine to supplement the erratic flow from the Bollin, the partners trialled the mule at Quarry Bank. In 1807 work began on a new steam-driven mule mill at Peter Street, Manchester. It cost the princely sum of £24,000 to build and equip; by 1811 it had 12,400 spindles, many more than Quarry Bank

Margins on cotton yarn were high for most of the war and both mills yielded good returns on capital invested, Quarry Bank averaging 18% between 1802 and 1811.

Speculation in land now became a feature of the Greg business. In partnership with William Hibbert, the brother of a Cross Street Chapel trustee, Samuel invested in land at Moseley Street and George Street in Manchester. That turned out badly when the anticipated development was deferred, but Samuel was more successful with agricultural land. In the early 1800s he purchased from the Earl of Stamford the whole Oak Farm estate to the west of Quarry Bank, followed by land at the village of Reddish near Stockport. But the Quarry Bank estate itself remained on leasehold.

Samuel matched his own father by producing thirteen children between 1790 and his 50th birthday in 1808. The boys attended Unitarian schools in Bristol and Nottingham and went on to spend some time at Edinburgh University, a Presbyterian stronghold which was then gaining prestige as a centre of radical thinking. All but the oldest, Tom, travelled in Europe to represent the company. Samuel and Hannah did not always see eye to eye as to whether the prime purpose of these visits was commercial or cultural. Nonetheless Samuel's willingness to indulge his wife's tastes for literature and the arts were admirably rewarded; despite having to cope with repeated pregnancies, Hannah proved an enlightened and energetic parent, always striving to broaden the education and experience of her family. Guests at both King Street and Quarry Bank, no doubt expecting the talk to be firmly rooted in business matters, would regularly be surprised at the cultured urbanity of the household Hannah had created.

Ellen Melly later recalled her mother's crucial role in the family as her children grew up. "In later years at Quarry Bank she was indefatigable in her endeavours to make all happy and comfortable; always ready to help my father, or at a moment's notice to accompany him to see after the farms and villages; and often on longer journeys; corresponding with her sons, and supplying their wants - cultivating their friends or those who might advantage them, for she had a great opinion of the educational value of good society, and her ambition was that wherever their lot in life might be cast, they might be sure to find some friend who had known her kindness."

In this and other contemporary accounts Hannah emerges as a remarkable personality in her own right. She was perhaps Samuel Greg's greatest stroke of good fortune.

Chapter 4

Risks and rewards on the high seas

Samuel's brother Thomas' early years in England are less well recorded. No individual portrait of this key family member has come down but he is thought to be the second from the right, between eldest son John and Samuel, in the Belfast family portrait. Much of what we know of him comes from his nephew, Robert Greg, writing much later. According to Robert: "He came alone to London (probably when about 15 or 16) to seek his own fortune; under what special circumstances I never learned, or why he chose the business of a Marine Insurance Broker". He added that his uncle "used to say he owed nothing to his family but an indifferent education".

Possibly Thomas harboured a grievance over his inheritance. He certainly enjoyed nothing to match Samuel's adoption by his maternal uncle, nor did he receive any direct inheritance from his father. However, his reference to the quality of his education at the Belfast Presbyterian school may have been unfair. These schools were often highly regarded, attracting the sons - and even a few daughters - of the well-to-do of all persuasions.

Among the pupils was Lord Hillsborough's daughter, Mary Amelia, who married into the Cecil family, became the first Marchioness of Salisbury and was a leading Tory hostess in the London salons of the 1780s and 1790s. Another pupil was Robert Stewart who, as Viscount Castlereagh, would figure as Irish Secretary in the formal union of Ireland with England and represent Britain at the crucial Congress of Vienna 1814/1815.

At sixteen young Thomas could hardly have "chosen" a career in insurance; rather his father must have chosen it for him, aware of the benefits to himself and his connections in Ireland of a son who was a

Member of Lloyds, which he is recorded as attending in 1772. In fact his father did his best to recruit clients for Thomas from among merchant connections all over Ireland.

The wars with France and Spain in the 1740s and 1750s added the danger of attack from enemy fleets and privateers to the traditional risks from storms and piracy, so there was a growing need for a more effective insurance industry. Yet marine underwriting before the 1770s was something of a free-for-all, with unrestricted access by gamblers and speculators to the business based on Lloyds coffee house, opened in 1691.

The Gregs and other Irish dissenting families - the Lyles, Batts and Cunninghams, along with the English Hydes, Philips and Hibberts of Manchester and the Rathbones and Lightbodies of Liverpool - were all involved in transatlantic shipping. Many would have known how it felt to lose ships or cargoes at sea without compensation, either because they had neglected to take out insurance or through the failure of the underwriter.

Thomas' nephew Robert again: "... by sundry letters he appears to have started on his own account as Insurance Broker, & Underwriter in 1772. He commenced with many good connections, his Father's House of Thos & John Greg of Belfast, Robt & Nath'l Hyde of Manchester, & the Philips, Hibberts & others...... The Business was first carried out in Lloyds Coffee House, then Old Bethlehem, Broad St, & finally Warnford Court, Threadneedle Street".

He goes on to describe the formation of a partnership called Thomas Greg & Co with a "cautious and clever Scotchman", George Wood, who continued as managing partner until Thomas retired in 1811. The name "Tho Greg, Merchant, 31 Old Bethlehem" appears in a 1775 London directory and "Gregg & Wood, Merchants, 31 Old Bethlehem" in a 1784 directory, with further entries in 1799 and 1804 at "25 Broad street buildings". In all the entries the description given is "merchant" or "merchants".

Chapter 4

Detail on the history of Thomas Greg & Co between 1772 and Thomas' retirement in 1811 is unfortunately missing, the relevant records having been destroyed in the 1840s. We do know that the intervening decades were times of rapid growth and change in England, not least in the City of London itself. This expanded the turnover of the partnership and developed its scope beyond marine insurance broking. Robert recorded: "This business had underwriting soon joined on to it, also general London money business, shares, loans, &c., and when my uncle retired, it was making £10,000/£12,000 a year".

Thomas Greg's early domestic arrangements in London are not clear, but he is noted as residing at Old Bethlehem in 1775 on premises comprising both living accommodation and a counting house or office, a normal arrangement. His unmarried sister, Mary, lived with him for a time. In 1780 Thomas married a slightly older woman, Margaret, daughter of Robert Hibbert of Birtles in Cheshire, reinforcing his connection with a family now prominent in London as well as Manchester. There were, however, to be no children of the marriage.

Thomas chose the right time to enter the marine insurance business. In 1771 Lloyds had become a society of subscribing members with a governing committee and rules. In 1773/74 it moved to new premises at the Royal Exchange, and in 1779 a standardised policy wording was introduced for marine cover. These and other changes combined competition between underwriters with a degree of structure and self-regulation, enhancing Lloyds' reputation and attraction for shippers and ship owners.

This mercantile prosperity had a darker side - the transatlantic slave trade.. Pioneered by Spanish, Portuguese and Dutch adventurers in the 17th century, it became dominated in the 18th century by British traders and ship owners.

It was these men who developed the "triangular trade", in which

European wares, particularly cloth and metal goods, were shipped from British ports to West Africa to trade against slaves supplied by local tribal warlords. The ships then transported the slaves to the British and French sugar islands in the West Indies, and auctioned them off to the planters. The planters supplied hogsheads of sugar, molasses, rum and other exotic island produce - all highly valued by the European consumer - to be shipped back to Europe, though not normally in the same vessels.

Meanwhile global events - the War of American Independence, closely followed by the Napoleonic Wars - were increasing the demand for marine cover. Between 1780 and 1800, Britain's overseas trade trebled. Premiums grew far more rapidly than volumes - hardly surprising when you realise that the first of these wars led to the capture of 3,386 insured ships. The Napoleonic Wars brought premiums up to £20-£30 per £100 of cargo value, and for "blockade runners" £40-£50 - fortunes of war indeed.

By 1800 Lloyds' membership had grown to 2000. After this a nomination process was introduced to weed out the dilettantes and punters. The aim was to restrict entry to men of commercial standing and probity, whether they were actual underwriters and insurance brokers or merchants and bankers.

Was Thomas astute in business or just lucky? Should he and "managing partner", George Wood, share the credit equally? How much capital the partners each held is unknown, but it seems likely that Wood's was much less than Thomas Greg's and that it would have been offset by Wood putting in longer hours, particularly after Thomas acquired land in Hertfordshire in 1783/84. In fact Wood was not elected to Lloyds until 1802, suggesting that until then had spent much of the time running the back office or counting house.

The other question is the relative roles of broking and underwriting in the activities of the firm. Later at Lloyds these became increasingly differentiated, but in the early years they were commonly combined. A focus on broking would accord with Thomas' father's original aim of finding reliable cover for the risks borne by the Greg family connections, rather than direct underwriting.

It would also have added to the success of the business. Brokers were powerful figures at Lloyds, because they controlled the competition between underwriters. You kept your premiums low - or lost the business to a rival. Thomas Greg & Co is estimated to have made total profits of £212,000 up to 1810, providing Wood with "an admirable fortune" as per Robert Greg by the time he retired.

Thomas's early success in business contrasted with the subsequent roller-coaster career of his father. As noted above, he cautioned his father against accepting a baronetcy offered by Lord Hillsborough which he had not the resources to support, and when Thomas senior lost money boring for local coal to fuel his pottery kilns, he turned to his son to bail him out, mortgaging to him his properties in the Belfast Quays. Much enhanced in value, they were inherited by his nephew, Tom, Samuel's oldest son. In those days uncle Thomas had the Midas touch.

As noted, Thomas' marriage to Margaret Hibbert produced no children, a circumstance that would have a large impact for the next generation.

The Hibbert connection

Calicos and slaves

In the 18th century the Hibberts' business based in Manchester was focused on overseas trade in finished cloth, including printed calicos from Calcutta. These products found a ready market, not only among Europe's well-to-do but as far afield as West Africa.

Slave ship captains were not just procurers of slaves but salesmen of goods supplied to them by merchants on up to two years' credit under sealed bonds, credit instruments equivalent to bills of exchange without the finite maturity date. They might spend months travelling between West Africa's coastal settlements and trading posts to dispose of their wares in return for human cargoes, the only means of payment available to the local warlord buyers. Textiles accounted for about half this merchandise.

So the original impetus for the Hibberts' involvement in the slave trade was their cloth business, and their role remained that of financiers rather than "slavers" in the sense of shipping human cargoes in their vessels. The arrangement had the key advantage that the substantial risks of the middle passage between Africa and the West Indies, including the incidence of death in transit among the cargo, was borne by shipowners.

Margaret Greg's uncle, Thomas Hibbert, had settled in Kingston, Jamaica, as early as 1734, to develop the business and receive slave consignments and settle accounts with the slave captains. He soon established himself as a slave factor or middleman between the slavers and planters in Jamaica and other islands. From the planters in turn he procured sugar and rum for shipment to London, where other members of the family established themselves as importers of sugar and other West Indian produce.

Chapter 5

For nearly fifty years Thomas Hibbert was a key figure in a family trading network that bestrode the Atlantic Ocean. Besides collecting payment in slaves against the bonds and procuring island produce on behalf of kinsmen in England, he was well placed to exploit the misfortunes that often overtook planters, whether from hurricanes, falling sugar prices or other causes. Over the years he acquired an interest in some 60 plantations mortgaged to him by proprietors unable to fulfil the terms of the bonds they issued in payment for slaves.

By these means Thomas Hibbert grew rich and powerful. In 1754 he acquired his own 3,000 acre plantation, and in 1756 he became Speaker of the Island Assembly.

Thomas had no legitimate issue of his own, but his success attracted several kinsmen from England. Of these his brother John Washington Hibbert, and a nephew died in their early twenties in Jamaica. However two nephews, Thomas and Robert, heirs to much of their uncle's fortune when he died in 1780, prospered. In the 1790s the profits of Jamaican plantations were aided by the slave rebellion in the French colony of St Domingue, then the largest sugar-producing area., triggered by the revolution in metropolitan France.

But they found the Jamaican climate harsh. While uncle Thomas had lived out his days in Kingston, they were pleased to leave their properties in the care of attorneys to retire to the temperate English shires. They invested their profits in landed estates, Thomas of Chalfont, heir to his uncle's main plantation, in Buckinghamshire and Robert of Birtles Hall, father of Margaret Greg, in Cheshire. Another Robert, born in Jamaica to John Hibbert in 1770, later settled in Bedfordshire.

The main progenitor of these nephews had been Thomas of Kingston's brother Robert, who produced eleven children in all. Aside from those already mentioned, the most important was George Hibbert. He found it politic to disown his family's dissenting background, went to Eton and on to Cambridge. He then joined an established partnership in London, trading with Jamaica. As this trade expanded, and with it his wealth, he invested in ocean-going vessels, becoming a member of Lloyds, a patron of the arts and a city alderman.

In the 1790s he promoted the formation of the West India Dock Company and became its first Chairman. With architect Robert Milligan as his vice chairman, he led the construction of the dock, built to receive and warehouse West Indian produce. It was opened in 1804 by the Prime Minister, William Pitt the Younger.

As a leading City figure, George Hibbert became a prominent protagonist for merchants and planter interests in defence of the slave trade, claiming it was essential to Britain's mercantile prosperity. When elected Member of Parliament for Seaford, he joined plantation-owning Members in defending the trade against Wilberforce and the abolitionists. Slavery had been made unlawful in England in 1772 and the slave trade was abolished in 1807, but the powerful planter representation in Parliament frustrated attempts to abolish slavery in British colonies for another 35 years.

George Hibbert's ships were engaged primarily in the direct trade between London and the sugar islands, carrying manufactured products for the plantations and returning with sugar, rum and other island produce.

Contrary to more simplistic interpretations of the triangular trade, slave ships themselves were not suitable for carrying perishable goods and generally returned from the sugar islands with timber or other speculative cargoes or in ballast. Thomas Greg's business with the Hibbert partnership in London was probably based on the insurance of these cargoes. However Guy Ewing, an early 20th century historian in the Hertfordshire village of Westmill, where Thomas settled in the 1780s, recorded that Thomas had found work for the village blacksmith in making tools "for his plantation in Jamaica", employing six men "to forge implements for the plantations in addition to the work required by the farmers of the parish".

While Thomas' connections must have given him many opportunities to invest in plantations, no mention of any property in Jamaica is made by his nephew Robert Hyde Greg, a meticulous recorder of all items of family property. Nor does Thomas' name appear in the large body of Jamaican records of proprietors of the time. Perhaps Ewing's report refers to the making of implements for the London Hibberts or other merchants for shipment to the plantations.

While there is nothing to suggest that Thomas harboured scruples about underwriting slave cargoes, they seem unlikely to have figured in his business with the Hibberts. Nonetheless, in the 18th century the slave trade and slave plantations were important in the emergence of a mercantile and financial empire the like of which had not been seen before. As already noted, Britain was in fact the first colonial power to ban the slave trade in 1807 and abolished slavery throughout her colonies 30 years later. This was not before they had contributed, albeit indirectly, to the prosperity of the brothers from Belfast.

A moral dilemma

John Washington Hibbert's second son, Robert, a man of considerable intellect and strong conscience, gives us an extraordinary example of the moral contradictions of the age. Born in Jamaica in 1770 he was despatched to England to be educated in a dissenting academy and went on to read law at Cambridge, where he fell under the influence of free-thinking clergy. This did nothing to divert his destiny from a career in business. In 1791 he returned to Jamaica to join the family partnership in Kingston. He married into a planting family, grew prosperous and bought a large plantation. Like his older cousins, Robert returned to England a rich man, and in 1805 he acquired the Hyde estate in Bedfordshire. Still in his thirties, he joined his Hibbert relatives in the London partnership. He also resumed his former Cambridge contacts. All this time a hefty income continued to flow from his plantation and its 500 slaves.

Chapter 5

His biographer, writing after emancipation, recorded: "....I was under the impression that this estate, like his other interests in the West Indies, came to him by inheritance. I now find it was not so and it is right to state that, though he was always a kind master, he had no repugnance to this kind of property on moral grounds. The explanation may probably be found in the belief that not only had slavery existed from time immemorial but was still considered indispensable to some extent".

However, Robert's Christian conscience was evidently not at ease. Now a convinced Unitarian, in 1817 he was persuaded by his Cambridge friends to despatch a Unitarian Minister as a missionary to his plantation. Was this the hypocrisy of an absentee slave owner? It was certainly naïve. The missionary in question, the Reverend Thomas Cooper, having fulfilled the three-year minimum term of his agreement, returned to report that the main impact of his mission at a time of growing unrest on Jamaican plantations had been to enrage fellow planters for arousing dangerous aspirations among the slaves. In particular, he had been forced to stop teaching the children to read.

Any moral dilemmas the Hibberts may have wrestled with were overtaken by the progressive decline of the profits from sugar, even before slave emancipation. Robert Hibbert's income declined after 1825 and he sold the Hyde estate in 1833 and his own plantation in 1836. The latter went for what was considered a knockdown price, though later events revealed it as a timely move.

Robert seems to have foreseen, and indeed welcomed, the abolitionist victory, and easily reconciled himself to a more modest lifestyle in Welbeck Street, London. Shortly before his death in 1847, having no children, he founded and endowed the Anti-Trinitarian Trust, renamed the Hibbert Trust after his death. The Trust Declaration instructed the trustees "to pay and apply the dividends, interest and income from the Trust Fund...... ..in such manner as they in their sole discretion shall.....deem most conducive to the spread of Christianity in its simplest and most intelligible form, and to the unfettered exercise of private judgement in matters of religion, and upon no other trust whatever".

While the word Unitarian does not appear in the Declaration or the Schedule of the Trust, this last sentence, with its implied rejection of conformity to orthodox doctrines, embodied the essence of Unitarian thinking and its intellectual orientation. In fact the resources of the Trust were used to provide scholarships which would develop a cadre of learned Unitarian pastors, drawn from carefully selected graduates of named Universities. Unitarians such as Mark Phillips and Robert Martineau were prominent among the early Trustees. The Trust and its Hibbert Journal has a long history in the English speaking world - it is still active today.

Thomas Greg had meanwhile remained close to his in-laws, whom he entertained at Coles, receiving £1,500 under the will of his father-in-law and a small legacy from wealthy Thomas Hibbert of Chalfont, who did the same for all his brothers-in-law. The death of his wife Margaret in 1808 did not weaken the family connection. George Hibbert, as well as his kinsman by marriage, was a client, a fellow member of Lloyds and, after his marriage to an heiress who brought him an estate in the parish of Munden in Hertfordshire, a near neighbour. But the Hibberts' wealth was in decline in the 1800s and George in particular had a large family with six daughters. One of them married his nephew and business partner, Samuel Hibbert, but Samuel died young, leaving his widow and two children in straitened circumstances. A childless widower by then, Thomas took her and her daughter into his own household and left her a property in his will.

London banker and country gentleman

An evolving banking system

The 17th and 18th centuries saw growth in commercial transactions with no corresponding expansion of the coinage. Merchants ran current accounts with trade partners fuelled by bills of exchange, with bills receivable their main current asset, other than stock, and bills payable their current liabilities. This made trade credit the main component of what we now call the money supply. For some merchants it was a short step to issuing promissory notes, attracting deposits from local wealthy people seeking interest on surplus funds and running accounts with tradesmen on which they could draw for local payments; in effect they were becoming bankers

Banks barely existed outside London before 1750, but they mushroomed under the impetus of economic growth as the century progressed. They reached their zenith in the period of cash suspension from 1793-1821, when, under the pressures exerted by high government borrowing to finance war spending, the Bank of England was relieved of the obligation to redeem its notes in cash.

The notes and drafts of the country bankers would circulate only in areas where their credit was known. Here, in fact, they were preferred to Bank of England notes. For payments further afield other instruments were required: cash, Bank of England notes whose issue was limited or bills drawn on accounts with known bankers located in London.

Drafts on London banks had a history going back to the 17th century, from which time local collectors would use them to remit rents to the accounts of the landed aristocracy with private West End banks. By the 18th century such remittance needs had widened through increases in overseas trade, taxation and Government borrowing. Merchants trading overseas, wealthy people, tax collectors and the country banks themselves maintained accounts with a "London Agent" who in turn kept an account with the Bank of England. This enabled them to handle non-local payments such as trade bills, taxation and stock purchases.

This informal three-tier banking structure sustained a rapid expansion of British commerce, national and international. It mobilised the surplus wealth of mature sectors of the economy for investment in the new capital-hungry mills and foundries of the North and Midlands and smoothed the flow of taxes and loans to the Treasury in London. Robert Greg's reference to "general London money business, shares, loans &c" shows that Thomas Greg & Co's activities extended beyond marine insurance to giving credit to his clients and providing other services akin to those of a banker.

This did not mean issuing notes. But Thomas' endorsement of bills drawn on Thomas Greg & Co by its account holders gave them the status of London drafts that could be used to settle non-local debts and be discounted for cash or Bank of England notes.

Given the blurred boundaries between general trading, banking and stockbroking, this was entirely consistent with the imprecise description of "merchant" which appeared against the name of "Tho's Greg" in the London Directories. This is supported by surviving account books of the post-1811 successor partnership of Greg Lindsay & Co. They show the firm having accounts with more than 300 persons or partnerships - "houses" in Robert Greg's parlance - plus the key feature of an account with the Bank of England, giving it access to cash and Bank of England notes for settling bills payable at maturity. These London banks also afforded their clients access to the burgeoning London stock exchange, whose first list was issued in 1801.

Chapter 6

So the Greg "house", located at Broad Street or later Threadneedle Street in the heart of the City, did not just bring together shippers and underwriters. It gave its clients access to other important financial services only available in London. Many of its accounts were with underwriters with London addresses, but they also included the businesses of the Greg family's mercantile and industrial connections all over Ireland and. England, Gregs, Hodgsons, Lyles, Batts, Warres, Hibberts, Rathbones, Philips and other merchants located in the provinces and in need of London's unique financial services.

When Thomas retired in 1811, times were still good for insurance brokers, underwriters and London banks. The driving forces were the war and the lax monetary conditions flowing from high Government spending and the dependence on short-term borrowing they engendered. It was this, aided by intermittent bad harvests, that drove up prices, rather than the suspension of cash payments blamed by the classical economists of the day. Between 1790 and 1814, wholesale prices are estimated to have doubled.

The old Usury Act of 1714 still limited the rate of interest on bills of exchange to 5% per annum. With higher returns available on floating Government debt not subject to the Act, wartime inflation made this ceiling a constraint on bank profits. As the war progressed, London banks shifted their focus from discounting commercial bills to investment in Treasury bills sometimes offering up to 17% on an annual basis, leaving discounting of commercial bills at the 5% ceiling to a new cadre of specialised bill brokers.

For bankers and others in the know who had surplus cash to lend to an impecunious government - the "tax eaters" condemned by Cobbett - the war therefore brought high returns. At the same time it engaged the whole nation as earlier dynastic conflicts had not, causing hardship for many. Aside from the sufferings of the combatants themselves, war-induced inflation raised the price of food and other necessities. This caused distress among the labouring classes, particularly when there was a poor harvest. The upper classes meanwhile faced unprecedented tax burdens, notably Pitt's income tax.

Napoleon Bonaparte famously disparaged England, the only European power he failed to subdue, as "a nation of shopkeepers". In fact history tells us that, in a prolonged war of attrition, it was as much England's financial muscle as her military prowess under Nelson and Wellington that overthrew him. Doubtless the usurper would have included the merchant and underwriter clients of Thomas Greg & Co within the compass of his jibe. But they too played their part in his downfall.

Farmer and socialite

As the profits of Thomas Greg & Co accumulated, the issue arose of how best to deploy his share for the benefit of present and future generations. The evolution from mercantile success in the City of London to landownership was already a longstanding tradition, one which went back to the days when impecunious monarchs granted titles and manors in return for ready cash - the origin of much of England's nobility. Later merchants were often happy to exchange the risks of fragile markets, theft, losses at sea and non-payment of debts, for the security of rent income.

So Thomas was following established practice when in 1783 he bought at auction the property of Coles Park in the Hertfordshire parish of Westmill for £3,137. This was to be his country seat rather than a source of income, but the following year he went on to purchase, for £5,250, the nearby Knightshill Estate. This was mainly freehold, with some copyhold land whose title rested on the record in manorial rolls. The Knightshill land was all leased to farmers.

The investment in land in the Westmill area continued. Against a background of rising farmland values, in 1802 Thomas spent £8,000 to acquire Tiller's End with 249 acres and Clinton's Farm with 25 acres. They were leased together at a total annual rent of £215. Further smaller land acquisitions followed, including in 1815 the purchase from the poet Charles Lamb of a property called Button Snap. By 1825 Thomas had accumulated a total holding of 1,481 acres, all in and around Westmill. Meanwhile he greatly extended and improved the Coles property and surrounding parkland, planting some fine cedar trees which can still be seen today.

Thomas began to spend more and more of his time at Westmill. He was a keen horseman and member of the Puckeridge and Buntingford Hunt. He also enjoyed shooting and kept a pack of beagles, all the characteristic pastimes of the landed gentry. As the largest local landlord, he established his status as squire of Westmill, a role to be retained by four further generations of the family. We have a few clues as to how villagers perceived their squire. Known locally as Grig rather than Greg, he was remembered by employees with affection as a character and a stickler for shutting gates. According to Guy Ewing, the historian, he had the only inn in the village, the Badger, demolished, because its location at the entrance to Coles "offered too much temptation to the servants of Coles and Rectory". Instead a house next to the church was converted to an inn, adorned with the Greg crest and renamed the Sword in Hand. It remains a popular watering hole today.

Thomas liked company. Perhaps because his own marriage was not blessed with children, he attached great importance to his family connections. He enjoyed entertaining his relatives and would eagerly welcome them to Coles, except for brother Cunningham.

His manner could be gracious and his hospitality liberal, whether for relatives, local personages like Dr Hicks of Buntingford and Mr Law, Rector at Westmill and Standon who liked a good wine, or grander folk. In particular he socialised with his former Belfast school chum Mary

Amelia, daughter of his father's patron, the Earl of Hillsborough, later Marquess of Downshire. She was now Marchioness of Salisbury and mistress of Hatfield House. He shared with the Marchioness a passion for fox hunting. He also lent her money - at interest - and said he would leave her a bequest in his will, though he never did so.

With the onset of war with France, Thomas' social advancement in the English shires faced a potential challenge as a result of his dissenting origins and the Irish connections on which his business had been founded. However, his adoption of the Anglican communion helped him to become accepted into English society and he was able to entertain the Duke of Bedford and Lord Brougham, the Whig lawyer, politician and subsequent Lord Chancellor.

Thomas developed an enduring friendship with Thomas Coke, owner of the Palladian mansion of Holkham Hall and vast estates in Norfolk and other counties which he had inherited from his great uncle, the first Earl of Leicester. Coke was MP for Norfolk for more than fifty years, eventually receiving the recreated Earldom of Leicester from the young Queen Victoria. History remembers him best for popularising the so-called Norfolk system of four-year crop rotation for turnips, barley, grass, wheat or similar crops.

Both men were dedicated to improving agricultural methods on their estates, but it was not all work and no play; the two Thomases also shared a love for hunting and shooting, and Coke was a renowned marksman. Coke promoted many improved methods on his estates. He introduced longer leases of 21 years, with covenants stipulating the practices to be followed. It was said that the annual rents on his West Norfolk estates increased from £2,200 in 1776 to over £20,000 forty years later.

Like Coke, Thomas looked on his purchases of tenanted properties as an investment and sought a better return on them than he could get on a bank deposit, mortgage or investment in government debt. However, higher rents had to be supported by better crop yields and livestock quality. The long leases and covenants were designed to give tenants incentives to reach these goals.

This period saw a huge upswing in farming rents, in response not just to better yields but also to other forces which are touched on below.

Enclosure of fields, previously divided into small strips under the medieval manorial system, had overtaken much of rural England, including Hertfordshire. A complex statutory process, enclosure was designed to consolidate farming into larger units able to support the investment in machinery and buildings needed to improve crop yields and the rearing of livestock. In the parish of Westmill earlier enclosures still left landowners with fragments of land which were less than ideal for efficient management. Thomas Greg was named with other landowners in promoting an enclosure bill in 1813 and was the largest allotee in an Award of 1819 .

Thomas did not approve of the local practices of ploughing four times a year and leaving land fallow one year in four. On the 240 acres he farmed for himself he developed his own system, designed to overcome the poor drainage in the heavy local soils. He would limit ploughing to once a year, with the type of plough and the method of operation meticulously prescribed. Ploughing had to be followed by the use of a scarifier and harrow to remove the weeds. This was all set out, together with detailed costings for comparison with other methods, in a pamphlet entitled "Mr Greg's System of managing a Considerable Farm in Hertfordshire" published in response to a request from the Board of Agriculture in 1809.

Thomas was something of an innovator as a farmer. He claimed to have introduced the yellow swede turnip to Britain as cattle feed. He experimented with cross-breeding cattle and with the application of lime to control pests in root crops. He was a keen exponent of mixed arable and animal husbandry, for the liberal addition of manure it afforded and he placed great emphasis on the importance of manure in raising crop yields. He acknowledged his debt to Coke, while noting that the heavy soils of Hertfordshire called for different methods from those used on the easily-drained terrain of Norfolk.

Arthur Young, in his 1804 survey of Hertfordshire for the Board of Agriculture, made many references to Thomas Greg. On the subject of planting in drills recommended by Townshend and Coke, he reported: "Mr Greg had tried it but gave it up as unprofitable on this soil".

Dr Hicks' son recalled Thomas' departures for Holkham through the streets of Buntingford as an annual spectacle. "He was seated in an open carriage drawn by four horses and two postilions in red jackets" he wrote. "The horses were the same as employed on the farm; they had long flowing manes and tails and looked very showy. Mr Coke used to pay him return visits and then there were high jinks at Coles".

The death of Thomas' wife Margaret in 1808 at the age of 58 adversely affected his manner towards others for a time. His nephew Tom Greg, Samuel's eldest son, who came to live with him at Coles while preparing himself for joining the London partnership, was often the victim of his uncle's black moods. Tom's mother, Hannah, claimed her brother-in-law would have been different if he too had had 13 children - an uncharacteristically barbed comment from someone normally sympathetic in her judgements.

Young Tom moved to the Albany in London in 1817, probably to the relief of both nephew and uncle. He later lived at Cork Street in London's West End.

Chapter 7

Aftermath of war

Financial crash

We have seen that the careers of Thomas and Samuel Greg followed very different paths after their arrival in England in 1768. Yet the brothers did not go their separate ways; family ties remained strong. Thomas' business had been founded on connections inherited from his father's mercantile activities in Belfast and his mother's family in Manchester, and his sister Mary supported him during his days as a bachelor at Old Bethlehem. We have also seen how readily Thomas welcomed his brother to Coles and how Samuel and his family exchanged visits with their Irish relatives.

These relationships of course extended to business. The Hydes were early account holders with Thomas Greg & Co, as was Samuel Greg and the other related families in Ireland and England.

By the time Thomas retired as active partner of Thomas Greg & Co in 1811, he had become at least as successful as his brother, despite the head start Samuel had been given by the endowment from his Uncle Robert. Now, having no son of his own, Thomas transferred his interest in the partnership to Samuel. His aim was to provide a business for his nephew, Samuel's eldest son, also named Thomas. This was all in the interests of the family's continued prosperity and position in the world.

George Wood also retired in 1811. He passed his interest to his nephew, James Lindsay, who had aristocratic connections, and his natural son, Thomas Walker, also referred to as Thomas Wood. He did not let go of the reins entirely - Robert Greg recorded that "G Wood was to continue to superintend".

Chapter 7

The new partnership took the name Greg Lindsay & Co, with capital split 7/12 to Samuel Greg, 3/12 to James Lindsay and 2/12 to Thomas Walker. The firm's profits stood at £6,300 in 1812 before nearly doubling to £11,181 in 1813. Samuel Greg's share was £3,670 in 1812 and £6,522 in 1813, without, it seems, his making much contribution to the business.

But the golden years of the new partnership proved shortlived. In son Robert's words: "At this time when my father joined, came the peace of 1814; and smash went all the old houses, and nearly all of Greg Lindsay & Co's customers, and the bad debts were frightful. Instead of my father coming in for £5,000 to £10,000 a year and a grand business for the eldest son Tom, he had to tax his own resources to prevent the total wreck of Greg Lindsay & Co".

History tells us that 1814-1815 was the time of one of the worst banking crises of the industrial revolution, thanks largely to the sudden halt in military spending at the end of the Napoleonic Wars. Though private banks had played a crucial role in economic expansion, they were generally undercapitalised. In contrast to the joint stock banks permitted in Scotland, they were also vulnerable to the death or withdrawal of partners. In the absence of any effective regulation, there was a great temptation to overextend, and linked liabilities meant that the failure of one bank would trigger other failures, loss of confidence, withdrawal of normal credit lines and a general downturn in trade. The vicious trade cycle of those times owed much to the banking failures excoriated by contemporary writers and politicians. They reached record levels in the three years from 1814-1816, when no fewer than 76 banks failed.

Robert Greg's account of the 1814 collapse and the years that followed focuses on the shortcomings and extravagance of Samuel's partners, James Lindsay and Thomas Walker. Surviving records show that they were both active underwriters. However it was surely an error for both the original partners to retire at the same time. Nor should they have overlooked

Samuel's inexperience of the City, his over-sanguine faith that the good times would continue and his preoccupation with his main textile business, which was facing particular challenges.

As the wartime continental blockade came to an end, Samuel had been persuaded to re-enter the Continental cloth markets in partnership with Isaac Hodgson, his wife's nephew, and warehouseman Garner Daniel. Unfortunately adverse exchange fluctuations, plus the confiscation by royal command of King Ferdinand of goods on consignment in Spain, led to losses of £32,000.

It seems unlikely that better foresight on the part of Samuel, brother Thomas or George Wood could realistically have prevented the "frightful" bad debts of the partnership. Bankers and their clients were faced with a financial meltdown, triggered by the cessation of wartime spending. All along the supply chains for war materials and support services, anticipated revenues vanished and bills drawn were dishonoured, bankrupting both the merchants and the bankers who gave them credit. Prices began to fall, and they carried on falling - for the best part of two decades. Inflation had enabled the London banks to prosper; in many cases, deflation proved to be their ruin.

It was too much for George Wood, and in 1817 he committed suicide. Robert Greg records further losses and heavy bad debts. Samuel Greg is recorded as "absent" and his son Tom, Robert's elder brother, who had joined the business in 1814, lacked experience and perhaps the necessary drive. When Walker retired the following year, £10,000 which he owed was written off and Tom took his place in the partnership.

In 1823 Samuel withdrew as partner, leaving only James Lindsay and Tom Greg. When the business finally closed in 1828, Lindsay owed it £7,576. He gave Samuel Greg, as ultimate creditor of the firm, interest-bearing promissory notes - which were never honoured.

By this time Thomas Greg senior had lost interest in the London business. Could he have stemmed its disastrous decline by exerting his authority as founder of the firm? From the failure of George Wood's "superintendence" over his kinsmen, it seems unlikely. Thomas apparently limited himself to carping at the inadequacies of his unfortunate nephew.

The textile empire expands

Samuel's cotton-spinning business was also severely damaged by the post-war slump. Alongside the Greg and Ewart partnerships' investment at Peter Street many other new mule mills had appeared in Manchester and other towns, some of them employing more than 1,000 people. Spinning capacity, so inadequate just a few decades earlier, was now over-expanded. The high wartime margins on yarn collapsed, and cloth exports were losing money into the bargain.

Samuel had no choice but to retrench. In 1815 he sold his interest in the Peter Street mill to Ewart, dissolving the partnership. Ewart took his mill into the McConnell & Kennedy partnership, familiar to Sam Greg as fellow clients of the Rathbones, whose eight-storey mill at Ancoats in Manchester had pioneered the harnessing of steam power to mule spinning. Built in the late 1790s, it specialised in the finer counts.

The break with Ewart was a defining moment. With a large family to provide for, Samuel Greg was in no position to retire as his older brother had with his fortune largely intact. The post-war recession lasted five long years, reaching its nadir in 1819. The 1815 sale to Ewart had been a timely move.

Samuel's firm now consisted of the Manchester cloth merchanting business, plus a single spinning mill with 4,000 spindles - well above the average capacity of the time, though quite modest compared to the larger mills then in operation. The heavy wartime investment in spinning capacity had reversed the previous imbalance between spinning and weaving and the industry now faced a growing shortage of weaving and knitting capacity.

These remained labour-intensive operations. Though Edmund Cartwright had obtained the first patents for his power loom as early as 1786-87, it was not until the early 1800s that the loom was successfully operated by manufacturers in the Stockport area, and it was not widely adopted until the 1820s. Rather than invest in such costly and unproven machinery, manufacturers preferred to assemble teams of handloom weavers in supervised weaving sheds.

Cotton cloth production was growing rapidly. Home-produced calicos were even displacing worsted and linen in some applications, and handloom weaver numbers were growing exponentially to meet the demand with the expanded yarn availability. One estimate suggests that in 1811 more than 200,000 workers were weaving mule and water frame spun cotton on the handloom, three times as many as in 1795. Even before the widespread introduction of power looms, the shift from a cottage-based industry combining spinning and weaving under one roof towards a more specialised factory-based model was well under way. The change separated spinning from weaving businesses and developed the active market in spun cotton yarns.

Weavers were not easy to find, and they could command high earnings. The closure of the Eyam weaving shed back in 1807 should be seen in the light of recruitment problems and the development of a ready market for good quality warp yarn at remunerative prices. After 1814 these margins declined, but Samuel Greg's commitment to the industry and belief that it would provide a future for the coming generation was unshaken. Despite his losses in the Spanish market, Samuel was better placed financially than many of his rivals. He realised that the expansion of spinning was likely to bring a shortage of weaving capacity, shifting profit margins in favour of weaving.

He was also well aware of the misfortunes of others. The related Hodgson family, for one, had been injured beyond repair by the disaster in Spain. Like Samuel, the Hodgsons had been endowed with a third of the Lightbody inheritance, yet they could not settle Isaac's debts to the partnership. Following father Thomas Hodgson's death in 1817, Isaac settled the debt by ceding to Samuel Greg his mill and landholding at Caton near Lancaster. Low Mill, driven by the River Lune, produced coarse yarn and was in need of modernisation. To supplement the unreliable power from the river, Samuel installed a steam engine and expanded the spindlage. But the operation remained vulnerable because it was a long way from the weaving centres.

In 1819, with no improvement in yarn profit margins, Samuel began the construction of a new four-storey mill at Quarry Bank, powered by a 100-horsepower iron wheel housed beneath the mill, with a tunnel to take away the tail water. This was a big advance in the engineering of water power and one which would keep it competitive with steam for many years. The investment sustained an expansion that more than doubled spindle capacity in the decade that followed; the workforce increased from 200 to 350. It clearly distinguished Quarry Bank from other first-generation water-powered mills, many of them abandoned through the bankruptcy of owners or the catastrophic fire damage to which cotton mills were notoriously vulnerable.

By the 1820s trade was recovering at last, and returns on weaving began to improve. In 1822 Samuel bought an old sail-making mill with cottages and land at Moor Lane in nearby Lancaster. Over the three years that followed it was converted and equipped with the newly-improved power looms to produce velveteens with warps supplied from Caton. In 1827 he followed this purchase by acquiring the Hudcar Mill at Bury, a steam-driven mule spinning and weaving mill, from the executors of its deceased owner, Thomas Haslam.

The investment over this period at Quarry Bank, Low Mill, Moor Lane and Hudcar totalled £240,000. This was a colossal outlay, even allowing for wartime inflation. Aside from a loan of £23,000 from Haslam's executors as part of the deal for Hudcar, plus a £5,700 partner's contribution from Samuel's son-in-law Andrew Melly, it was all financed from retained profits. Finally in 1832 the partnership acquired Lowerhouse Mill at Bollington, Cheshire, a former silk mill, part water and part steam powered, which Samuel Junior re-equipped in the following years. At that point, with Caton and Lancaster forming a joint unit, Samuel had a mill to pass on to each partner son.

The partnership accounts reveal that returns on capital invested from the four mills reached nearly 30% in 1822/23 and again in 1823/24, before slumping to minus 9.5% the following year. This was typical of the roller-coaster trade cycle of the times. Nevertheless they averaged 11% over the 11 years 1820-1831, amply confirming Samuel's perceptions back in 1819.

This was a remarkable feat, especially so late in life - Samuel reached 70 in 1828 - but it is doubtful if he could have done it without the support of his sons. Robert and John managed the mills respectively at Quarry Bank and Lancaster with nearby Caton, but Robert also spent much time and energy supporting his father in the Manchester merchanting business. The fortunes of this part of the enterprise were mixed, with export markets incurring heavy bad debts from 1819-22 and again in 1829. After this the Manchester business stopped selling cloth and yarn for other mills except on commission, which left the credit risk with the principal seller. Instead they focused on the greatly-expanded output of yarn and cloth from the company's own mills.

Even in the 1830s, most cotton firms were small. New entrants to weaving with power looms would rent not just space - often taking a single floor of a mill - but access to water or steam-driven power. Of nearly a thousand textile firms in England, only a handful could match Samuel Greg & Co's combined spinning and weaving capacity.

But there were no great advantages or economies of scale to be reaped from the multi-mill structure. While the output of yarn and piece goods was all sold by the one Manchester merchant house, slow communications made joint decision-making difficult. Each mill could best be managed by someone on the spot, typically a resident owner-manager. The drive to expand to several locations was mainly driven by Samuel's desire to provide viable businesses for his sons.

Though the Greg mills remained in the ownership of the company through the 1820s, the four sons were progressively taken into the partnership with endowments of £5,000 each of their father's capital, starting with Robert in 1817 and ending with William in 1827. Some devolution of management was achieved by leasing the mills at the appropriate time for the appointed son to manage, in return for rents to their father in respect of a valuation of the buildings and machinery which represented his investment. This devolved approach was no doubt the best way of tackling the management problem, but it was accompanied by some tensions between father and sons. Robert in particular had his own ideas about the future of Quarry Bank and the company.

The mills were treated as separate profit centres and each son had the incentive of knowing he would in due course inherit the mill he was running. Nevertheless the overall profits were divided between the partners, regardless of their mill's performance, on a formula based not on profits but on their respective age and experience. In 1831 Samuel took 40%, Robert 25%, John 15% and Samuel and William 10% each.

Although the partners' rewards turned on the company's total profits, there was no central board or policy-making function to maximise profits or resolve disagreements; Samuel remained the sole authority. Such a patriarchal regime placed great dependence on the continued health and competence of the father, a common frailty in family businesses.

The late 1820s brought particular problems for Quarry Bank. Under the Greg & Ewart partnership it had established a reputation for high-quality coarse yarn, much of it sold in niche markets, especially in the Norwich area where it enjoyed good margins. After the war these margins never recovered and the partnership's investment in looms at Lancaster and Bury proved crucial to overall returns. But in 1825 came another banking crisis. Quarry Bank began to make repeated losses and Robert disputed the valuation placed on the mill for the purposes of fixing the rent.

In 1831 Samuel finally called for an independent valuation by his former partner, Peter Ewart, with John Kennedy of the firm of McConnel & Kennedy, who was related to the family through John Greg's marriage to Elizabeth Kennedy. The valuation confirmed Robert's contention, finding that the mill was overvalued by 52%. Samuel senior nevertheless resisted pressure from his son to introduce looms at Quarry Bank. Nor would he countenance buying cheaper raw cotton to improve margins.

The argument over raw cotton at Quarry Bank casts doubt on the degree of proper devolution of management to the next generation. In 1828 Hannah Greg died. With her death an important force holding the family together was lost.

Now 71 and widowed, Samuel was depressed by old age and inactivity. In 1831 he wrote to Robert: "I feel my powers of body and mind rapidly in decay - I know that age and youth cannot feel and think alike. I see my opinions without influence and I wish to avoid the occasions of advancing any".

Samuel retained control of the business for too long. He did not retire as an active partner until 1832, and even then it took an accident which left him lame and immobile to force the issue. By the time he died in 1834 he must surely have felt he had long since achieved his goals in life, especially that of providing an apparently solid future for all his sons.

Chapter 8

Wills and inheritance

For most of England's population, the main impact of the wars with France had been higher food prices and rents. We noted the spectacular increases claimed for Thomas Coke's rents over the years from 1776 to 1816.

Improved agricultural methods were only part of the story. Thomas Greg's land acquisitions were timed to yield the early windfall gains experienced by landowners in the war years, when corn prices, unchecked by imports because of the blockade, reached high levels, particularly in years of poor harvests. Contemporary accounts dwell on the suffering among the landless labouring classes when harvests failed. The high farm profits and increased rents were the subject of contemporary comment and criticism from many, including the poet Byron, who excoriated in verse the rapacity of landlords at a time when war had demanded sacrifice from so many.

It is hard to quantify precisely the various causes of the wartime escalation in produce prices and rents and the associated boom in land values. Was the major factor rising consumption spurred by population growth, the war blockade, successive years of poor harvests, excessive issue of banknotes or pure speculation? Perhaps each of these contributed.

Acts of enclosure, which called for considerable investment by landowners, accelerated under the incentives of high produce prices and rents. This was despite high interest rates on mortgages and government debt, which in more normal times would have discouraged them. In contrast to earlier enclosures, which had reduced the number of farmers, the high profits of the 1790-1811 boom years sustained their number. Some however had to borrow heavily on mortgage to cover enclosure costs and invest in buildings and machinery, producing a debt burden which would prove insupportable in less buoyant times.

It may well be that by 1814 improved farming techniques, along with heavy investment and better management flowing from enclosure, had brought food production back in step with population growth.

The abnormal conditions of war and poor harvests only served to defer an inevitable fall in farm prices and profits. This made nonsense of the theories of David Ricardo, leading political economist of the day, who claimed that population growth was bound to drive prices ever upwards as cultivation was extended to more marginal land.

Meanwhile the Board of Agriculture found that higher wartime prices were accompanied by rising costs. For example, on a typical large arable estate with increases in taxes and poor rates, costs rose by 90% between 1790 and 1813.

When the war ended, the landed classes who dominated Parliament sought to extend the good times via the Corn Law of 1815. This virtually prohibited imports unless wheat rose above 80 shillings a quarter, a level unthinkable back in 1790, though imports continued to play a small part for many years afterwards.

Though relieved of the burden of income tax, farmers had to support further increases in poor rates just as prices and profits were falling. This left those who had borrowed heavily in serious financial difficulties. Coke himself pleaded in Parliament the case for relieving hard-pressed farmers from the twin burdens of land tax and rates.

No detail of Thomas Greg's rent income has come down, though he did later assert that he had lost money by going into land, which he had done from a sense of public duty. Those sentiments were echoed by the many who participated in the frenzied land speculation of the war years. It is quite possible that twenty years later the values of some of the land he had acquired in the 1790s and 1800s had fallen below the prices he had paid. Nonetheless, following the reversal in prices, he appears by the 1820s to have been looking once again for better returns on accumulated cash than he could obtain in the funds, the equivalent of today's gilt-edged securities, or from a bank deposit.

In his early seventies Thomas plunged money back into farmland; this time, on Coke's advice, in distant Norfolk. Neither the costs nor the circumstances are clear, but we do know that in 1825 he bought four large farms, total 924 acres, in the north east of the county, some twenty miles from Holkham. Though forming one consolidated landholding, they touched three separate parishes - Gimmingham, South Repps and Trunch.

With 83% arable land and 10% pasture, this was evidently productive ground for cropping. Surveying the locality back in 1804, Arthur Young had written: "About North Walsham a mixed soil, that is, a sandy loam; some sand; and the sub-soil sand"; clearly a contrast to the conditions at Westmill. While the vendor is not known, it is tempting to conclude that it was sold in one lot by some over-indebted grandee or his executors, possibly through the good offices of Coke. Thomas' strong cash position is attested by the Land Tax assessments for his new properties, for which he was "exonerated" for having paid up front. Four years later he lent £1,000 to Admiral William Windham at 4.5%, secured on a 100-year mortgage on 98 acres in nearby Gresham. Nothing further has come down about these lands except the early surrender in 1845 of the mortgage to the Admiral's executors, and in 1851 the sale of the whole of the entailed Norfolk estate for £33,400 by agreement between Robert Hyde Greg and his eldest son, Robert Philips Greg.

This consent was required to break the entail, a restriction on inheritance discussed further below, on the Norfolk estate in order to fund the acquisition of the freehold to the Quarry Bank estate. That sum was realised at a time when the purchasing power of money had risen by 80% to 100% since 1815 as the inflation of the Napoleonic war years was reversed.

Chapter 8

Thomas of Coles lived for twenty-four years as a childless widower. After the loss of his wife his situation at home was eased, and his moods doubtless improved by two of her relatives. Mrs Sam Hibbert, one of George Hibbert's many daughters and widow of her cousin Samuel Hibbert, moved to Coles with her daughter Anna to superintend Thomas' household. Visitors commented favourably on the new régime and the graciousness of the ladies. Thomas would later leave Mrs Hibbert a life interest in Mundesley Cottage, a substantial property on his Norfolk estate. Her son, Samuel, became one of his executors and continued to live at Mundesley until his death in 1867.

Thomas' younger sister Eleanor Warre, described as "a strong minded clever lively woman" by her nephew, Robert Philips Greg, was another frequent visitor. Her son Henry, elected to Lloyds in 1819, became Thomas' favourite nephew - so much so that some thought he might even displace the less favoured Tom Greg as his heir. To their uncle's gratification, no doubt, Henry Warre married Anna Hibbert.

No history of successful families of those times can overlook the subject of inheritance and marriage portions. Status and security for the propertied classes depended crucially on these endowments or expectations of them. They were especially vital, as we have seen from Samuel Greg's career, as a business resource at a time when capital in business was largely personal.

Inheritance could also breed dispute and disharmony. Thomas of Belfast's will had caused a huge rift when Cunningham, his third surviving son and business partner in Belfast, convinced his father on his deathbed, in his brothers' absence in England, that the partnership could not survive a large withdrawal of the father's capital. Thomas had been thinking of the plantation Thomas and Samuel had inherited from his childless brother John the previous year. "Whereas my brother John having provided for my sons, Thomas and Samuel, I bequeath all my property to my son, Cunningham" ran the text.

Chapter 8

But John Greg's bequest to Thomas and Samuel had been subject to his widow Catherine's life interest - and she survived a further 24 years. By the time she died in 1819, according to Robert Hyde Greg, "the property had become comparatively worthless".

The underhand nature of this episode outraged the disinherited brothers. Although Samuel later made peace with Cunningham on condition that he gave £1,000 each to the unmarried sisters and £800 to the married ones, Thomas pronounced him a "scoundrel" and never spoke or wrote to him again.

Samuel had in fact done better than Thomas. Their father had a year earlier given him his half share in his land in New York State "as a place of retreat into a free country or a Provision for a son on a future occasion". The wording is doubly significant. First there is the inference that Ireland, or even England, in 1796 was not "free", at least in matters of conscience. Second is the implication that Samuel was being favoured on account of the sons he would need to provide for, in contrast to son Thomas, still childless after eight years of marriage. Father Thomas also urged Samuel to buy out Waddell Cunningham's half-share, which he did.

Cunningham Greg evidently earned an unsavoury reputation for contesting wills. Much later in 1830, when he complained to Samuel of Thomas' refusal to reply to his letters, Samuel responded brusquely, noting that, in addition to his role in their father's will, Cunningham had even contested their uncle's original bequest of the Hillsborough plantation.

Even the reversionary interest in the plantation was to prove a vexation for Thomas. In 1802 his aunt Catherine, John Greg's widow, obviously seeing him as the nephew with the deepest pockets, began pestering him for money. From her comfortable home in Hampton, south London, she wrote to plead misfortune brought on by a hurricane in distant Dominica, promising generous future returns on a modest present investment. Thomas' response must have been suitably hard-nosed; she later complained that she had been 'forced to accept' the conditions he imposed. In 1813 she was back for more money after another hurricane destroyed the dwelling and slave living quarters at Hillsborough.

We are reminded of that remark by Thomas that he "owed nothing to his family but an indifferent education". Did he have a genuine chip on his shoulder, as the oldest surviving son, at being been short-changed over the family patrimony, or did it reflect a belief that his success was entirely down to his own efforts - something brother Samuel, beneficiary of his Hyde uncle and recipient of a £10,000 marriage portion, could hardly claim?

When the brothers finally gained possession of the plantation in 1819, Thomas sold his share to Samuel in return for a £1,500 annuity. This suggests not so much a disdain for slavery as caution, born perhaps out of the fate of Greg Lindsay & Co, towards property outside his scrutiny and control. He may also have received some sound advice on the poor outlook for the price of sugar.

Either way, Samuel became a slave owner for the last fifteen years of his life. When the legislation of 1835 freed slaves throughout the British colonies, his son Tom would receive £5,000 compensation for loss of property, that is the slaves in his ownership. The Hillsborough plantation would eventually pass to Robert Hyde Greg's grandson, John Tylston Greg.

Landowning families usually made family settlements to prevent their estates from being split up among several heirs. Keeping the estate together also served to perpetuate and enhance the family name and standing. Aristocratic families also had to support titles, landholdings and associated patronage and power, which often included seats in the as-yet-unreformed House of Commons. Younger sons of the titled classes were found appropriate callings - church, armed forces, even trade - while forming a "reserve team" in case the heir should die without male issue.

Samuel's wealth was industrial rather than landed, and he always resisted his son Robert's urgings to buy out the freehold of the Styal estate. He had already made it clear that his other four surviving sons should inherit the mills they already managed. In effect his estate was split up during his lifetime.

Thomas' estate, by contrast, was largely in land and property. Though he had no child of his own to pass it to, he followed the practice of the landed classes of holding it together through a settlement, entailing his properties in Hertfordshire and Norfolk on his brother and thereafter his oldest nephew. The entail was a legal condition in a will restricting the inheritance of property to the oldest male descendant. Breaking the entail required the consent of that descendant.

No record of either Thomas or Samuel's will has survived. However Samuel's grandson, Robert Philips Greg, who inherited the entailed estates, wrote later of his great uncle: "Old Thomas Greg left about £130,000 including the Herts and Norfolk estates" and of his grandfather: "A nice courteous old gentleman, he left about £230,000, I believe". How much credence can be given to these figures is not clear, though we do know that the author responsible was meticulous about money values.

While the numbers suggest that Samuel made a larger pile than Thomas, his estate presumably included the entailed Hertfordshire and Norfolk properties inherited from Thomas, so his £230,000 would have included a portion of Thomas' £130,000. These numbers should be multiplied by something like one hundred for comparison with 2010 values.

Comparisons between these two remarkable brothers are inevitable. Samuel's contribution to the early cotton industry was large enough to be significant to the English economy itself. A courageous, even incautious, entrepreneur, he made some big mistakes, yet he was nonetheless capable of what we today would call strategic thinking. He also brought to his

Thomas Greg, 1718-1796

Thomas Greg of Belfast 1718-1796 & family

Samuel Greg, 1758-1834

Hannah Greg 1766-1828

Robert Hyde Greg 1795-1875

Edward Hyde Greg 1827-1910 & Sons

business a prodigious energy and organising ability. Age had not diminished his powers by his sixties, when he backed his judgement with high-risk investments. He left to his sons a large and thriving concern.

Full credit must also be given to Hannah's support over nearly forty turbulent years. Through it all they remained a modest and unpretentious couple compared to brother Thomas and later generations. A businessman first and last, Samuel kept a low public profile. His achievements went largely unrecognised, in his lifetime or later.

Thomas by contrast was a cautious pragmatist who believed that who you knew was more important than what you knew. He shunned uncertain ventures, preferring to leave the risks to others while he played the role of judicious lender and creditor - a natural banker, if you like. A man of persuasive charm, he was adept at securing clients and cultivating connections. None of his descendants moved in such elevated circles. If the pun may be excused, Thomas was the most gregarious of the Gregs.

He nonetheless contributed to the emergence of Lloyds of London as the world's premier market for marine insurance, and played a role in the agrarian revolution. Whether he was sagacious or just lucky he timed his key moves well, to finish up with a handsome fortune of his own making. With the exception of Cunningham, he remained close to his own and his deceased wife's family and friends to the end.

Thomas died in 1832. He was buried in the family vault at Westmill with his wife Margaret; his nephew Tom joined them later.

Thomas' funeral was long remembered in Westmill for its old-fashioned pomp. A tablet in memory of Thomas and his wife stands in the church, close to those of two later Greg squires, Robert Philips and Thomas Tylston, and their wives.

Samuel died two years later, in 1834. He was buried with Hannah at the Parish Church of Saint Bartholomew in Wilmslow, in a vault originally set up for two of their children who had died young and for Samuel's unmarried sister, Jane. His funeral was attended by more than 500 people, mainly tenants and employees.

Chapter 9

A new generation

The offspring of Samuel and Hannah Greg had an auspicious start in life. The genetic inheritance of such remarkable parents, the quality of the Unitarian schools of the time and Hannah's committed and enlightened approach to her children's upbringing combined to promise success and fortune.

The England of the early 19th century was still very much a male-dominated society, yet this did not prevent the women of Hannah Greg's household from playing significant roles. The influence of "the ladies" at Quarry Bank has already been noted. While three of Hannah's daughters, Elizabeth Rathbone, Hannah Reynolds and Ellen Melly, helped to cement the family's business connections by marrying well, Marianne and Hannah stayed at Quarry Bank to support their mother. In the 1820s they promoted the Oak Chapel and the welfare of the Styal community, work which was carried on after Hannah's death.

Of the five brothers who reached adulthood, the oldest was Thomas (Tom) Tylston Greg, born 1793. As already noted, he had been adopted by his uncle, Thomas of Coles. The timing of his entry to his uncle's business was as unfortunate as the uncle's had been providential. His business career, however, suggests that he lacked the qualities that brought success to his father and uncle - he certainly cannot have had much appetite for hard work, as he retired at thirty-five. This he could well afford after his father's death in 1834. As the heir to his uncle's entailed estate he lived on unmarried, content to manage the Coles estate, where he made various improvements.

Tom had also inherited his father's West Indian plantations, just before the emancipation of slavery throughout Britain's colonies. The properties were already suffering from falling sugar prices when in 1834 they were devastated by a hurricane. He wrote to Robert that nothing remained of the estate but the shape of the buildings, which he later reported he could not afford to restore. As noted above, he received £5,000 from the Treasury in compensation for loss of property. He died in 1839, still in his early forties.

The remaining four sons, Robert, John, Samuel and William, all followed their father's calling by entering the Samuel Greg & Co partnership. Robert was six years older than John and much older than the younger two. His longer experience lent him greater weight with his father, reflected in the distribution of the firm's profits, which made him at least first among equals following the father's death.

After older brother Tom's death, the other brothers were no longer his equal in a more tangible sense, due to his inheritance, as Samuel's oldest surviving male heir, of their uncle's entailed estates. Like his father before him, Robert Hyde Greg was the great inheritor, able on several occasions, when less well-endowed brothers fell on hard times, to buy out their shares in the patrimony.

Frailties of a family company

The 1830s saw renewed expansion in the cotton industry, driven by advancing technology on several fronts. Earlier inventions, especially the steam engine and the power loom, had become much more efficient and reliable. By 1835, more than 100,000 power looms were in service.

The same decade saw the widespread adoption of Richard Roberts' self-acting mule, an innovation which over the years would significantly increase the optimum scale of spinning mills. In the early 1820s, with Crompton's mule having superseded the water frame as the main spinning machine, most mills in Lancashire had employed no more than 100 to 200 operatives. With its manually-operated carriage the mule called for the strength and skill of a grown man, so these spinners became an exalted cadre with semi-independent status. They employed their own assistants and enjoyed piece-rate earnings far above those of other operatives.

The hand mule's effective capacity was however limited to 250-280 spindles and many of the new "self-actors" were made by modifying hand mules that could then be operated by semi-skilled spinners within existing floor space. However the full potential of the technology called for much heavier investment, not just in machines with up to 800 spindles but also in larger mills to accommodate them.

With yarn and cloth prices in decline and other costs broadly unchanged, the only way to improve profits was to increase productivity. If a spinner with two or three assistants could somehow operate a pair of mules with 16,000 spindles instead of just 500, the investment would pay off handsomely. This, however, would mean a new generation of mills. Such was the scenario faced by the four brother partners in Samuel Greg & Co in 1834.

As previously noted, while father Samuel had focused on preparing them for business, their mother Hannah had encouraged them to follow more intellectual pursuits, from literature and art to the sciences and even politics.

Of the four, John perhaps most closely matched his father's single-minded dedication to business. Low Mill at Caton, to which he was assigned, was a "can of worms" from the outset. Launching the new operation at Lancaster in the 1820s, when his father was already an old man, called for drive and tenacity.

At the other end of the spectrum, William Rathbone Greg, the youngest son, was very much an intellectual. When the manager of his mill at Bury departed, it seems he lacked the drive to take control of operations and keep the mill running properly.

Chapter 9

William and his brother, Samuel junior, shared an aspiration to improve the physical and moral condition of workers. In the rapidly-growing manufacturing districts this left much to be desired, thanks to overcrowding, bad housing, poor sanitation and, especially, addiction to drink. Both men became founding members of the Manchester Statistical Society, which carried out a series of surveys into living conditions in and around the city. Between 1833 and 1842 they contributed reports on a range of subjects, from criminal and medical statistics to education and factory inspection reports.

The rough and tumble of the political world, however, never appealed to Samuel junior. A pious man, he held an ideal of an industrial community in which relations between employer and employee would be in permanent harmony. In the Lowerhouse Mill project at Bollington he saw an opportunity to give tangible form to his dream. It was not to be. Samuel's early enthusiasm for a plan to convert the former silk mill for cotton spinning was to prove utopian, and yield unfortunate results.

Robert Greg managed to inherit in equal portions the talents of both parents; his mother's devotion to learning and the arts and his father's business acumen. In later life, business would prove the winner. As a young man, however, he shared the interest in nature and landscapes that inspired the Lake poets, also studying the architectural treasures of Europe and classical antiquity.

These predilections, along with his wide knowledge of history and the classics, are evident in his journals of travels in Scotland and Spain in 1814/15 and France, Italy, Switzerland, Greece, Turkey and Austria, the more conventional grand tour, in 1817/18. The relevant manuscripts have fortunately been recovered by Allen Freer. Faithfully transcribed and edited by him and his wife, Beryl, they were published in December 2007. The text is illustrated by some of Robert's sketches of scenery and buildings, the sole recording method before the advent of photography.

The journals convey the impression of an exceptionally learned young man thirsty for new sights and experiences. In an age when travel either by land or sea was hazardous and uncertain, he was endowed with considerable drive and physical endurance.

In some respects Robert appears a product of the romantic revival, the age of Wordsworth, Byron and Goethe. At the same time his journals include much hard data - dimensions of length, width, height, weight and distance, even population figures, all set out in clear readable prose. For example, how many travellers have assessed and reported, as he did, the annual consumption of candle wax in the cathedral at Seville converted to tons?

The journals clearly show us the two contrasting sides of Robert's nature; the lover of nature and the arts and the bean counter. It was this close attention to accounting detail that would characterise his business life.

Robert returned to Manchester society much fortified by his travels. Unsurprisingly, given his business prospects, he married well. His chosen bride was Mary Philips, the daughter of a prominent Manchester Unitarian family. He soon began to acquire a public profile never commanded by his father. He became prominent in the Literary and Philosophical Society and joined the city's Chamber of Commerce, serving a term as its president.

His interest in education extended to the working classes. With Benjamin Heywood, he became a founder of the Manchester Mechanics' Institute, set up on the model of the institutes pioneered by George Birkbeck in Glasgow and London.

In the mid 1830s, his connections, reputation and communication skills, along with his prominent role in the cotton business, made him a natural spokesman for the Anti-Corn Law League which campaigned for the abolition of the duties imposed on imports of corn. These duties raised the cost of food for mill workers and other town dwellers when harvests failed for the benefit of landowners.

From this he was drawn into politics. His brother-in-law Mark Phillips already held one of two Parliamentary seats in Manchester created by the 1832 Reform Act. In 1839 Robert was nominated by Richard Cobden, leader of the campaign against the Corn Laws, for the other seat, which had become vacant through the retirement of Poulett-Thompson. Though facing a strong Tory candidate in Sir George Murray, one of Wellington's former generals, he was elected, despite being absent abroad at the time.

A somewhat reluctant legislator, Robert joined his brother-in-law in representing the emerging metropolis of the north and its manufacturing interests. He also succeeded Poulett-Thomson as President of the Anti-Corn Law League.

This was to prove the high-water mark of his public life. A factor in his advancement had, of course, been his status as senior partner in Samuel Greg & Co, of which a contemporary wrote: ".....the firm of Samuel Greg & Co holds first rank among the manufacturers. It consumes annually nearly four million pounds weight in cotton, possesses five factories, four thousand power looms and employs more than two thousand people at Bury, Bollington, Caton, Lancaster and Wilmslow".

Yet this mighty company was beset by problems. Margins were improved at Quarry Bank with the introduction of self-acting mules, but performance at the Hudcar Mill at Bury deteriorated after 1832, when William's manager was transferred to support Samuel at the startup of the Bollington project. Then in 1837, a fire destroyed much of Low Mill at Caton and threatened the operation at Lancaster, with its dependence on Caton warps.

Robert's absence overseas in 1839 was necessitated by stress and exhaustion. He had been working desperately hard to combine his League politics with the challenge of leading the partnership through these setbacks. Given these distractions, and remembering his tendency to pay too much attention to detail, his leadership could not really match his father's. It did not help that the company's profits turned on the contributions and commitment of all the partners and these were becoming conspicuously uneven.

1841-42 was a year of acute depression, and the company suffered heavy losses. Faced with the choice between active politics or family commitments, Robert chose the latter. He resigned his Parliamentary seat in 1841.

The same year, he took the lead in the breaking up of Samuel Greg & Co. Each brother took his own mill, though until 1844 all retained their interest in the marketing arm in Manchester. It was an amicable separation and a timely one; the problems at Bury and Bollington were threatening to drag down the more robust parts of the business. The break-up was initially a matter of book keeping - working out how profits and losses should be shared - and the brothers continued to hang together, conscious that in the eyes of the industry, and of Manchester society, they were still a single family business.

The commercial need to pull together, as much as brotherly love, brought them to Samuel junior's aid when he hit stormy waters in the 1840s. Heavy investment in housing and other facilities for his workers at Lowerhouse Mill had brought him to the brink of bankruptcy. There was clearly some sympathy for him; in 1832, not only the mill itself but the whole village of Bollington had been virtually derelict. Workers had to be brought in from Styal and Wilmslow, and many cottages built or rebuilt to get the project off the ground.

In retrospect this was a risky venture, and one which called for great determination as well as stringent cost control. But Samuel would never allow the bottom line to obstruct his vision of a happy community. His grandson Osbert Greg recalled: "This village seems to have been the forerunner of Garden Cities, since each cottage had its own flower and vegetable garden amounting to some eight roods each. He built playgrounds and Sunday schools for the children and organised evening classes and parties for the employees....... The girls' and boys' schools together contained some three hundred and the teachers consisted solely of the men and women employed in the mill..... He also started what surely must be the first instance of factory Bath and Washhouses". Samuel participated personally in community activities, especially teaching in the Sunday school.

The role of the enlightened, benevolent employer was not easy to reconcile with the tough choices that had to be made in the face of difficult trading conditions. In 1846 Samuel's workers went on strike over the introduction of new tentering machines. This was not a particularly unusual incident, but Samuel, feeling he had done so much to help his workforce, took it as a personal betrayal.

It proved a psychological blow from which he never recovered. Samuel withdrew from the business, turning his back on an industry where he had sought to be the model employer. He became something of a recluse, living the rest of his life at The Mount, the house he had built at Bollington.

Both Samuel and his wife Mary went on to publish books on religious topics. In 1857 they entertained the Hungarian revolutionary Lewis Kossuth at The Mount. Their elder son Herbert, an athlete and sportsman, went into the cotton industry and ultimately joined the sewing cotton business of James Chadwick & Bros at Eagley, near Bolton. Younger son Walter trained in the law and became a partner in Orford Cunliffe Greg & Co, the Manchester legal practice which looked after the legal needs of later Greg generations.

Turning to the youngest brother, William Rathbone Greg's lack of commitment to business was not helped by the poor health of his first wife, Lucy. After 1842, when they moved to Ambleside in the Lake District in the hope of improving her health, he attended Hudcar Mill only on a part-time basis. In 1847 he seems to have abandoned Hudcar to follow a slightly quixotic urge to rescue his brother's business at Bollington. That mill was saved, but Hudcar continued to make losses. Eventually, in 1850, William sold it for £17,000, a paltry sum compared to the price his father had paid. However the exit from the industry proved a turning point; it freed William to devote himself full time to his literary career.

The break-up of a company

So by 1850 Samuel Greg's great enterprise had crumbled and only two of his sons remained in the industry as mill owners. What had gone wrong? Was it an example of the weaknesses of the partnership structure in managing a large enterprise? Industrial leaders were still selected by the random chance of kinship, the driving force in partner capitalism. The history of Robert & Nathaniel Hyde underscores how vulnerable a business can be to the death of a key partner. For an enterprise to survive you need a son, or least a nephew, as successor, though an outsider equipped with the necessary additional capital or expertise was a possible alternative.

The early business success of Samuel Greg and his brother Thomas turned crucially on the contributions of their partners, respectively Peter Ewart and George Wood. As in the case of Greg and Ewart, the structure could be tailored to some extent to recognise and reward knowhow as well as capital, but the fundamental principle remained – each partner was expected to contribute inherited capital, management input or an appropriate combination of the two. The weakness of the system was that it gave no weight to other key factors - personal interest, commitment, and an ability to meet the demands of management.

The cotton industry continued to change. Prices and margins were increasingly set by larger mills than those the brothers had inherited in 1834. Robert and John nonetheless retained their faith in the trade on which the family's wealth and standing had been founded, and saw it providing a future for their own posterity.

They were of course well aware of the changes; the new model of larger spinning mill, the role of doubled yarns in specialised warping and knitting applications, and the margins on power loom weaving. In the 1840s returns at Quarry Bank were improved through the installation of looms. To the chagrin of his brother William who believed the revival at Lowerhouse Mill had been due to his own efforts, John took it over as senior partner, with a view to providing for his sons, Francis and Albert. Meanwhile, freed from the burdens of public life and leading the old partnership, Robert was aiming to match his father by providing separate mills for his sons to manage and ultimately inherit.

In 1847 Robert rented a six-storey spinning and doubling mill at Calver in Derbyshire for his eldest son, Robert Philips Greg. Formerly owned by the related Pares family, it was powered by water. Calver's output was designed to meet the demand for doubled yarns for lacemaking in Derby, Nottingham and Leicester. Over the following fifteen years, Robert invested heavily in re-equipping it.

He made his second son Edward Hyde Greg, a year younger than Robert Philips, a partner in Quarry Bank itself. In this case, Robert continued to exercise close personal supervision of what was still his largest working asset. However he seems to have recognised its limitations as an ageing rural mill with poor transport links, whether for raw materials or finished output. In most years market prices for its yarn, taking into account delivery costs, were unremunerative, and spinning output was confined to the mill's own requirements for weaving.

Once the investment in power looms of the 1840s was completed, capital spending at Quarry Bank stayed modest for the rest of Robert's life. While national cloth production continued to grow, Quarry Bank's output stagnated.

Chapter 9

Investment at Reddish and the 1860s recession

The attention of both Robert and John Greg focused instead on the potential of their father's estate at Reddish, south of Manchester, which had originally been split equally between the five sons. Here there was plenty of land for development, along with canal access from the Lancashire coalfield for the supply of coal for steam raising. The low cost and reliability of steam by contrast with water power was becoming increasingly evident.

Reddish had all the advantages their father's old mills had lacked - a reliable energy supply, easy access to the market and a plentiful supply of adult labour. Nonetheless, the brothers' experience of the early 1840s downturn had bred a cautious approach.   In 1847, rather than encumbering themselves with the risks of expanding their own yarn capacity, they began the construction of two spinning mills, patriotically named Victoria and Albert, on adjacent sites, for lease to third-party tenant entrepreneurs.

Unfortunately the cotton spinner at Victoria, a man called Ogden, quickly failed and the mill was sold. Bowlas, the spinner at Albert, also ran into difficulties. It was initially as Bowlas' partner that wealthier brother Robert involved himself in the Albert Mill, bringing in his own capital to double its capacity. On Bowlas' retirement in 1853, he assumed control in partnership with his third son Henry. By this time the mill was larger than Quarry Bank and could accommodate the latest spinning and doubling frames. Of all the family's mills this was to survive longest, as an independent trading concern under the name of R Greg & Co.

Renting mills as Ogden and Bowlas did was a common enough practice, but their experience illustrates the problems arising from the treatment of cotton mills and other fixed assets created by the industrial revolution as pieces of real estate capable of paying fixed annual rents. Remember the dispute in the 1820s over the rent Robert's father had charged for Quarry Bank. Such rents failed to reflect the high risk attaching to such assets, with earnings subject to heavy swings between profit and loss. This aspect of the sole owner or partnership model of enterprise contributed to the high incidence of business failures. However, with one brief exception, the Gregs were to cling to the old model till well into the 20th century.

Robert Phillips Greg described the £15,000 cost of Calver Mill as his own "half share" in the proceeds from the sale of the entailed Norfolk estate. But it turned out to be the least successful of his father's ventures. Despite further investment in machinery to produce specialised doubled yarns, the mill was never profitable and it was sold in the late 1860s.

Robert senior had faced the same dilemma as his own father in trying to build a multi-mill business, the mixed abilities of several sons. He attributed the failure of Calver to his son's incompetence as a manager, yet the warning signs had been all too evident from his time working in the Manchester marketing business. But it went very much against the grain for a proud captain of industry to accept that his son could be unfit to run a mill.

The later history of John Greg and his family is not too clear. We know John upset his brother William by taking over Lowerhouse Mill at Bollington for his son Francis to manage and inherit. Francis and his brother Albert then formed a limited liability company under new legislation to run Bollington with additional capital from Rathbone, Melly and Greg shareholders.

In the early 1860s the whole industry underwent severe recession. On top of this, cotton shipments from the Confederate states were suspended during the American civil war. Mills some distance from the main markets and the coalfields, or which relied on water power, generally had lower margins due to advances in steam technology, and suffered disproportionately. Quarry Bank weathered the storm, but John sold both his mills to Storey Brothers in 1864 and Francis sold Bollington the same year. From there on the family's connections with the industry were largely in the hands of Robert and his descendants.

Was Robert's survival in these hard times due to shrewd judgement, or simply a longer purse as inheritor of his uncle's entailed estate? It was that resource that had helped him to acquire the freehold of Quarry Bank, Samuel and William's share of the Reddish land and, later in 1873, that of John himself. The land at Reddish became a key asset.

Chapter 10

Politics and industrial relations

The first Samuel Greg had shunned politics; typical dissenting businessmen of his generation believed it was a field best left to aristocrats and landowners. No record of his opinions has come down, even on issues like the tariff reform that so affected his business. The social and political significance of Samuel's role as a large employer in the new factory system may never have crossed his mind.

This was not true of his sons, especially Robert and William. Both supported the 1832 Reform Act, which redistributed seats in favour of the new industrial towns and extended the vote. In later life, however, they had grave reservations about its further extension to those without property.

William's career was another illustration of the problems of the large family business. He was a man condemned to a calling for which he was temperamentally ill suited. Sharing with his brother Samuel a strong social conscience, he was also an astute observer of the wider political and economic issues that prolonged warfare and the 1815 restoration of the old monarchies had put on hold. In England these were Catholic emancipation, Parliamentary reform, the Corn Laws, tariff reform and factory regulation.

A talented writer, William gained public attention in 1842, at the age of 33, by winning a prize offered by the Anti-Corn Law League for the best essay on the subject of "Agriculture and the Corn Laws". However his literary career was for some time constrained by business setbacks and his efforts to rescue his brother Samuel from his troubles at Bollington, and was not helped by his wife's illness.

Chapter 10

After William lost his mill in 1850, his journalistic and literary talents were free to blossom. His book *Creed of Christendom*, published in 1851, gained him some standing as an author, and he began contributing to quarterly magazines, widely read by the Victorian intelligentsia, on political and economic issues of the day. On the death of Sir Robert Peel, the first industrialist to be Prime Minister, his essay on his career in the *Westminster Review* was judged the greatest contemporary tribute to the statesman's life and work..

Following his first wife's death William moved to London, where he was able to move in influential circles while supporting himself somewhat precariously from his earnings as a journalist. In 1856 his connections won him a Commissionership of HM Customs, giving him the security of a £1,200 annual salary. In 1864 he was elevated to the post of Comptroller of HM Stationery Office.

These were not sinecures and he complained of the tedium of daily attendance at the Board of Customs. But he acknowledged that the work was less than arduous. However, in contrast to latter-day civil service posts, these positions did not debar him from engagement in political controversy. Publications continued to flow from his pen. Titles included *Political Problems of our Age and Country (1870), Rocks Ahead*, or the *Warnings of Cassandra (1874)* and *Mistaken Aims and Attainable ideas of the Working Classes (1876)*. His political and social judgements were conservative, and he remained steadfast in resisting extensions of the vote to the working class.

In 1849 William had written an article in the Manchester Guardian criticising the widely-acclaimed novel Mary Barton by Elizabeth Gaskell, wife of the minister at the Unitarian Chapel in Cross Street. The book had described working life in Manchester in the early 1840s but William complained that it unjustly maligned the cotton industry employers. The issue was the more poignant for being fought between prominent Manchester Unitarians.

Nonetheless William's writings were characterised by balance and urbanity and he became an opinion former for serious readers among the mid-Victorian well-to-do. Collections of his essays were published and re-published, both during his lifetime and after his death in 1881.

William's role in politics remained that of an observer and commentator. We have already seen how Robert participated in the campaign against the Corn Laws, and won and then resigned a seat in the reformed House of Commons. However Robert remained prominent as a mill owner and employer, in which role he is mentioned, for instance, by the German revolutionary, Friedrich Engels, in his 1844 book *The Condition of the English Working Class.* This was in part a diatribe against the new rich bourgeoisie of "manufacturers" as exploiters of their workers, in contrast to the bourgeoisie of the pre-industrial era, who had acknowledged an obligation to support their journeymen and artisans. Engels confidently predicted an English revolution led by this new "proletariat".

Almost anywhere else in Europe censorship would have ruled out publication of such a subversive message, but in the event Engels' predictions proved massively wide of the mark. England escaped the 1848 wave of revolutions that engulfed most of continental Europe. Engels acknowledged his error in a later revised edition.

The original version presented Robert Greg as the personification of the paternalist cadre of employers who, in Engels' perception, beguiled their operatives into loyalty and docility by providing cheap housing, free education, chapels, Sunday schools, and so on. Engels claimed that such workers were thereby "enslaved", particularly by the provision of housing. He was particularly concerned by the challenge paternalist employers such as Arkwright, Strutt, Owen, Ashworth and many other rural mill owners besides the Gregs presented to the whole concept of class war which he and his mentor, Karl Marx, were propagating.

The controversy focuses attention on the employment practices at Quarry Bank in particular, which was one of the last mills to abandon the recruitment of Poor Law apprentices. The original mill had relied on child labour for half its workforce. When the second mill was built in 1819-20, the workforce expanded towards 350 and the proportion of parish apprentices dropped below 40%, though it was still a high figure. Nonetheless £6,000, nearly a fifth of the total cost of the expansion project, was spent on the construction of forty-two cottages to house the adult workforce, along with a manager's house.

In the 1830s the mill continued to struggle to find enough adult labour, especially when it was obliged to provide key workers for the Bollington startup, when some families on poor relief from as far away as Oxfordshire were brought in. Robert carried on building and by the 1870s he owned 108 cottages housing more than 500 people. These were built to a higher standard than the urban homes of textile operatives, where overcrowding and poor sanitation were the norm.

We know Hannah Greg had a hand in Samuel's attempts to develop Quarry Bank as more than a place of work, with a shop, a chapel and a school. Robert, as a young man of liberal sympathies, strongly supported his parents' philosophy. In the 1820s his interest in improving the skills of male workers had led to his helping to found the Manchester Mechanics' Institute, and he promoted another in Styal to improve the skills and understanding of science among his own employees. He encouraged societies of various sorts, including a debating society.

After his father's death and the resignation of the Unitarian minister, Robert appointed another Unitarian, John Colston, as Minister of both Norcliffe and Dean Row, a chapel he had restored. He nonetheless recognised the preference among his employees and tenants for a less intellectual form of worship, and had a wagon shed converted into a Methodist chapel.

These practices all made commercial sense to the paternalist mill owner in terms of trouble-free labour relations. Disputes over wages and working conditions in the 19th century cotton industry were widespread and took on all the features of class struggle, at least in the urban centres.

Chapter 10

There was usually fault on both sides. A downturn in trade would lead to wage cuts by employers, which led to protests, strikes and lockouts. The unrest led Engels to label downtrodden cotton operatives as class warriors, and to portray England as ripe for revolution.

The Gregs, however, believed that the labour market should be free and unregulated; they condemned new factory legislation as state interference. Robert's role in the League made him a principal exponent of free trade and the laissez-faire principles behind it. In truth he failed to see the inconsistency, while opposing duties on corn, raw cotton and other articles of commerce, of his stance in favour of an export tax on textile machinery as a defence against foreign competition. He strongly opposed the Ten Hour Movement, which led to the 1833 Factory Act limiting the hours women and children were permitted to work. In practice this legislation was widely evaded.

Samuel and William, for all their social conscience, agreed with their brother about restrictions on working hours. Their first contribution to the Statistical Society was a report asserting that the conditions in the cotton mills were much better than had been reported by the researchers who had been gathering evidence to support the new legislation. In general the Gregs opposed anything that constrained the freedom of the employer, especially the activities of the unions which from time to time had tried unsuccessfully to recruit their workers. In taking this stance, however, they overlooked the less benign practices of some of their fellow mill owners.

Robert was not a man to overlook the importance of the 'bottom line' at Quarry Bank in favour of social experimentation, any more than his father was. Both generations imposed strict discipline on their workers; the appointment of a doctor for the apprentices was as much to check their physical capacity for work as to treat their ailments. Truant apprentices were chased up and punished, and fines imposed for misdemeanours and poor work. Costs were controlled by paying wages at piece rates per unit of output and the rates were generally lower than those in most urban mills. It was a harsh régime, but it did result in much-valued security of employment and low rents for homes which were spacious by the standards of the times. The workers could buy fresh food cheaply from Oak Farm, and their cottages had sizeable gardens which yielded plenty of home-grown produce. Living standards at Quarry Bank were therefore at least equal to those of the urban workers. This and the healthier lifestyle are reflected in low staff turnover and sickness absence.

Robert's commitment to the workforce and their families was demonstrated during periods of short-time working, when lower piece-rate earnings were partially offset by reductions in cottage rents. An ex-employee later recorded that during the American Civil War, when a failure of raw cotton supply forced the mill to close, men were found alternative work on the estate. Youths were sent to school at the employer's expense and women organised into a sewing school. In a reference to Robert and his partner son, Edward, he wrote: "The Greg family did nobly in furnishing employment for all their factory employees. In fact anything to tide them over hard times without humiliating their pride". This was an eloquent commentary on the Gregs' role as employers in the 19th century, a tradition that would be continued in the next.

Hard times continued to be frequent. The mill's profitability fluctuated with the ebb and flow of the textile trade cycle, but the success of Robert Greg's employment policies and the loyalty of his workers, in some cases successive generations of the same family, offset the disadvantages of location in the relatively remote Styal. Operations at Quarry Bank were stopped by industrial action only once during the 19th century, during the Plug riots of 1842, when militant Chartists from Stockport managed to bring the mill briefly to a halt. Similar policies were followed at the Albert Mill with equal success.

Chapter 10

Robert Hyde Greg's inheritance and legacy

Robert's later relationship with his father was characterised by differences over the question of the direction the company should take; subsequent events would in general back the younger man's judgement. Father and son nevertheless shared a common belief in the cotton industry, and a commitment to it.

The 1841 dissolution of the old partnership had freed Robert from the burden of trying to resolve the disparate agendas of his brothers. After his brother Tom's death in 1839 he inherited his uncle's entailed properties in Hertfordshire and Norfolk, giving him the option, at 46, to retire from business altogether, as had both his uncle and his older brother, and live the life of the landed gentleman. There is no evidence, however, that he ever entertained such a move. Instead he saw his inheritance as a means of sustaining his ambition, after the example of his father, to provide viable businesses in the shape of cotton mills for his own sons.

He achieved this for two of them, Edward Hyde Greg at Quarry Bank and Henry Russell Greg at Reddish. The youngest son, Arthur, was more successful in business than either of his brothers. He joined James Chadwick & Bro, the sewing cotton firm in Bolton, eventually becoming Chairman of the Board. His success owed something to his freedom from his father's often overbearing tutelage.

Kinship was still the most powerful element in selection and promotion in business. Arthur's cousin Herbert Greg followed him into Chadwick's, as did Edward's second son, Ernest, in the following generation. But this was one of the new model joint stock companies which facilitated the split between ownership and management, something the Gregs in general were slow to adopt.

For all his commitment to the industry, Robert was equally attentive to the family's interests in land and property. One of the issues with his father had been the freehold of the Styal estate, which Samuel had persistently declined to acquire. As his approach to development at Reddish showed, Robert's experience of bad times made him aware of the risks involved in cotton manufacture. He saw the need for diversification of the family's wealth into the more secure income from rents.

As a young man, Robert's interests had extended to agriculture. Like his uncle Thomas, he set great store by improvement and raising returns, and he applied these principles to the estates he inherited. Instead of moving to Coles Park following his brother Tom's death, he let it to a tenant. In 1848 he built himself a new neo-gothic mansion, Norcliffe Hall, near Quarry Bank, while his son Edward and family occupied Quarry Bank House.

Robert and his wife Mary were frequently seen at Westmill, where he was recognised as the village squire. They created a second home at Knightshill. Dubbed "the cottage" within the family, it was in fact a substantial residence with extensive land. On the expiry of the lease, Robert farmed there himself with the help of his own bailiff, always taking a close interest in performance and investing heavily in new buildings.

He wrote a long letter to the Manchester Guardian in 1842 on the subject of farming in the Scottish Lothians, a model he had studied and admired. Subsequently published, it included this tribute to his uncle's farming expertise: ".......my farm is in the county of Hertford and consists of 500 acres. It is conducted on the best system current twenty years ago, superior to anything in these parts and my bailiff was brought up in the Lothians".

Robert invested further capital in 1849/50, replacing the old residence at Coles with a mansion on similar lines to Norcliffe while he continued to let the property to the existing tenant, a Mr Soames. He supervised the construction of both Norcliffe and Coles personally, paying close attention to their design and cost.

When the Soames tenancy ended in 1871, son Robert moved into Coles with his wife Louisa, née Gair, solving the problem of his inadequacy as a businessman. His father wrote to him: "I have no doubt that to become a country gentleman would, on the whole, conduce more to your comfort and happiness than remaining in business in Manchester". From this time on Robert senior became known in Westmill as "old Mr Greg".

By the middle of the century Robert held freehold property in Hertfordshire, Norfolk, Reddish and, having bought out his brother Samuel's quarter, a half share in two plantations in the West Indies. However at Styal, except on the Oak Estate, the land was on a lease which would terminate on his death. He felt he had to remedy this, regardless of cost. Capital was also needed to support investment at both Calver and Reddish. The entailed Norfolk estate continued to yield rent income, but the capital it offered was now more important. As mentioned above, in 1851, as part of the deal to acquire the Calver mill, the entail was broken by agreement with his eldest son, Robert Philips Greg and the Norfolk land sold; it fetched £33,400. Also sold in 1853 was the land in New York State, for a modest £3,377. Robert Philips Greg's Recollections records that this money was bestowed on his brother Henry as a coming-of-age present. In 1855 these resources finally enabled the family to acquire the freehold of Quarry Bank, which would prove a valuable investment for later generations.

Robert's focus on the consolidation of landed wealth and the construction of mansions was accompanied by a conscious pursuit of family status. More than a century after their migration from Ireland, the family had always felt the need for acceptance in English society. Thomas of Coles, the squire of Westmill who hobnobbed with the aristocracy, flaunted the family crest from which the Sword In Hand public house took its name, and had it embossed on his carriage.

For the benefit of himself, his brothers and their male issue, Robert's last act before he died was, at some expense, to petition the Lyon King of Arms for Scotland for a Patent of Arms based on descent from Scots nobility. The Patent, granted posthumously, rehearsed Robert's descent firstly "from the clan Gregor who after the proscription of his family and name assumed the surname Greg and settled in the County of Ayr" and secondly from his maternal grandfather, Scots-born Adam Lightbody, whose childless brother William had borne arms. This right accrued to Adam and, in the absence of male issue, passed under the laws of heraldry to his co-heiresses. The next generation of Gregs obtained from the Garter King of Arms for England the right to add the further Tylston quartering based on Adam's English wife Elizabeth, née Tylston, whose forbears had also borne arms. Tylston was added as a second baptismal name to several generations of male Gregs.

The Scottish descent was authentic insofar as we know Robert's great grandfather, John Gregg or Greg, had been born in the parish of Ochiltree. So was the proscription of the Macgregor name, reinstated by the 1774 Act of the Westminster Parliament. It is nonetheless curious that, as noted above, the Gregs' forbears in Scotland and Ireland were Presbyterians, presumably descended from the Covenanters so mercilessly persecuted by the restored Stuart dynasty. As such they would have been staunch supporters of the Hanoverian succession, whereas the clan Macgregor remnants seem to have been Jacobites who fought with Bonnie Prince Charlie in the '45 rebellion.

The history and culture of the clans had of course been much glamorised by Sir Walter Scott and others since the ill-fated uprising, and they enjoyed the patronage of royalty from the day in 1821 when George IV donned a tartan kilt over his portly frame to visit Edinburgh. Naturally the office of the Lyon King and their client Edinburgh lawyers will not have allowed such subtle quirks of history to prevent them from taking their due fees.

Other than Tom, the oldest son, those of Samuel and Hannah's children who reached adulthood all lived on into their seventies or eighties.

Chapter 10

Their lives spanned a period of British industrial and commercial dominance, spearheaded by the industry in which they were so prominent. Nonetheless their history underscores the precarious nature of partnership capitalism in the Victorian era, even for well-established families like the Gregs.

Competition was fierce and the trade cycle vicious. Engels described the aspiring industrialists as "people eager to make fortunes, industrial Micawbers and speculators, of whom one may amass a fortune while ninety-nine become insolvent, and more than half of the ninety-nine live in perpetually repeated failure". It was true that for many the spectre of bankruptcy was always around the corner - witness the efforts made to help Samuel Greg junior to stave off disaster in a society dedicated to upholding the rights of property at all cost.

As we saw, Robert was the only son and partner in Samuel Greg & Co who did not succumb in one way or another to the competitive challenges of the industry - and even his survival owed something to an inheritance from non-industrial wealth. Nonetheless the second generation had many admirable traits as individuals, Robert and William gaining a level of public recognition during their lifetime that their father never managed.

Robert left the bigger mark. He was a cultivated man of wide interests and an enlightened employer who was alert to the needs and aspirations of his workers. Though business worries blighted his early enthusiasms, his attachment to beauty, natural and man-made, remained - as the gardens at Quarry Bank, now restored, demonstrate. He was also a man of strong if selective affections, most notably for his mother, his wife and his daughter Caroline, whose early death at 37 came as a great blow.

He was less successful in his relations with his sons, particularly his eldest, Robert. Their mutual disregard was a source of lasting distress to his wife Mary. It was Henry with whom Robert achieved the most fruitful working relationship. Henry wrote to his older brother after their father's

Henry Russell Greg & Family

Earnest William Greg 1862-1934

Henry Philips Greg 1865-1936

Alexander Carlton Greg 1902

death: "I daresay you will miss Pater's coming to Coles and conferring on matters with him and also feeling that the cottage is quite deserted. Pater was certainly a most reliable rallying point and one always to be depended upon, giving stability to all around him". A positive enough endorsement, though not exactly overflowing with filial affection.

Robert Hyde Greg's prominence was in some measure a matter of his birth, but would not have been achieved without sound judgement and vision to go with it. Over a long business career that spanned several crises in the cotton industry he inherited, preserved and consolidated wealth, rather than creating it. He faced tough choices in business, but, with the exception of the Calver project, most of his judgements turned out to be correct. He managed to steer two of his mills through the competitive challenges of the 1840s and 1850s, as well as the cotton famine of the 1860s on which Calver and the mills of his brother John and nephew Francis foundered.

Robert died in 1875, aged 79. He was buried not with his parents but in a new family vault at the Unitarian Chapel at Dean Row. He is commemorated at Westmill by a memorial window in the church. He was survived by several siblings: Samuel until 1876, William until 1881, John until 1882 and Ellen until 1894. According to the record of his eldest son his estate was valued at "about £230,000 gross", a similar level to that of his father's four decades earlier.

Diversification and disposal

A 20th century man of letters

After 1875, the family records focus mainly on the posterity of Robert Hyde Greg. However his brothers John and Samuel junior also had issue, and their sons have been mentioned above.. His youngest brother, the author William, also had sons, Percy and Eustace, by his first wife Lucy. In 1874, after her death, he married again, to Julia Wilson, who gave him another son, Walter Wilson Greg. By this time William himself was sixty-six and his son Percy already thirty-nine.

Both Percy and then Walter followed their father's literary bent, Percy primarily as a journalist on the *Manchester Guardian* and other journals. He also wrote a history of the USA, some five novels and a little poetry. His writings did not however match his father's, often expressing extreme opinions which shifted substantially over the course of his career.

William himself died in 1881, leaving his widow and youngest son, still an infant, in somewhat straitened circumstances. Much of Walter's youth was spent wandering around continental Europe with his mother. However, the experience made him an accomplished linguist, and he inherited journalistic talents from both parents, along with valuable connections. His maternal grandfather, James Wilson, had been founder and first editor of *The Economist*, and the publication remained a Wilson family business with a son-in-law, Walter Bagehot, its third editor.

Walter Greg had himself been designated for the editorship after graduating from Cambridge, but his interests lay in literature rather than economics. He turned down the post to devote himself to the study of literature and bibliography. Another gregarious Greg, he moved easily in academic circles, both in his own country and overseas. In all he had over 700 articles, commentaries and studies published, on many literary subjects. He became President of the Bibliographical Society in the early 1930s and was known as an authority on the subject throughout the English-speaking world. Late in life, his expertise was acknowledged by the award of a knighthood. Sir Walter Greg died in 1959 at the age of 84.

Slow decline of Quarry Bank

Robert Greg's early retirement stratagem for oldest son Robert Philips Greg turned out well. He proved a benevolent and respected full time squire at Westmill and presided over the estate for 35 years, pursuing his interests in minerals and languages and publishing books on both subjects. He extended his property interests by buying out the quarter shares in the West Indian plantations held by his hard-pressed uncles John and William, but like previous generations, remained a strictly absentee landowner. He sold the Cane Garden plantation on St Vincent in 1870 and in 1894 the Hillsborough plantation to his nephew, John Tylston Greg, son of brother Edward, who settled there and remained an active planter until 1928.

For the descendants of Robert Hyde Greg still involved in the cotton industry, the years after 1875 would be a period of slow but remorseless decline. Progressive social, economic and fiscal changes proved inimical to family businesses, the textile industry in England and inherited wealth generally.

Robert's estate - two working cotton mills, extensive real estate and liquid cash - was broadly split between his four sons, Robert Philips, Edward Hyde, Henry Russell and Arthur. Robert Philips' share included the entailed Hertfordshire estate he already occupied. Quarry Bank and Albert Mill passed to Edward and Henry respectively as their personal properties. Both continued to be run on the partnership model, though trading under their existing names as Robert Greg & Co and R Greg & Co. However, the flaws in that model which had affected both their father's and their grandfather's businesses remained.

Of Edward Hyde Greg his son, Alexander, wrote: "Whilst neither Samuel Greg nor his son Robert Hyde Greg ever had any particular relaxations or hobbies, my father had many and diverse ones..... He was also a very keen soldier, but as fate had not destined him to join the army he had to be content with the auxiliary forces of the 50's and 60's and joined the Cheshire Yeomanry."

Edward's "fate" was to be a mill owner, heir to Quarry Bank and a large portion of the village of Styal, including Norcliffe, a handsome enough inheritance. Norcliffe Hall with its park was a more fitting home for a man of substance with a large family than Quarry Bank House, cheek by jowl with the noisy mill. The mill itself would prove more of a liability than an asset; its turnover dropped catastrophically from the late 1870s to the turn of the century. The main cause of this was a series of reductions in overseas markets as European governments fostered their own cotton industries, using heavy tariff protection to keep out Lancashire's products.

As a single rural mill, Quarry Bank was poorly placed to compete. It suffered persistent losses and short-time working. The Gregs could no longer guarantee employment to their workforce, and the prosperity of the whole village declined. In the late 1880s an attempt was made to improve competitiveness by replacing some mule capacity with ring spinning frames, especially suitable for coarse yarns, but the impact was marginal. Spinning, the sole activity of the original mill of Samuel Greg, was discontinued entirely in 1894.

Edward's control at the mill had officially begun in 1870 when his father retired. In contrast to earlier generations at Quarry Bank, he was content for most of his career to wring his hands about his business and focus on his "relaxations and hobbies". He preferred hunting and shooting, cutting a dash in Cheshire society as a JP, county councillor and Deputy Lieutenant. He sent his sons to expensive schools. His marriage in 1856 to Margaret Broadbent, "a beautiful, accomplished and witty woman" according to their son Alexander, produced six sons and two daughters.

This fourth generation of English Gregs was affected by the demise of the Unitarian private schools that had nurtured their parents. Never a chapelgoer, Edward was happy to follow the Victorian upper-middle-class practice of sending boys to the new breed of public school modelled on Rugby, created by the Anglican Dr Arnold. Two of his sons went to Rugby, while the others attended the slightly less prestigious Repton. The oldest, Thomas, went on to Oxford.

Edward found his sons' education a large expense. He complained: "fate ordained a nursery of twenty years coinciding with business losses for over ten years".

Hard times did not cure Edward Greg's vain and extravagant ways. Having rented out Quarry Bank House, he was reduced to mortgaging Norcliffe to maintain his lifestyle while he waited for something to turn up. Fortunately for him, the fates were kind. Neither of Edward's wealthy brothers, Robert and Arthur, managed to produce an heir. In the face of the new death duties Edward had waived his right to succeed to the entailed properties in Hertfordshire, so they passed to his eldest son, Thomas Tylston Greg, as next in line. His brother Arthur, Chairman of James Chadwick & Bro at Bolton, helped out by employing second son, Ernest. Arthur later propped up his impecunious brother via the Norcliffe mortgage before dying in timely fashion and bequeathing the property back to him.

Son Alexander recorded: "Arthur Greg died in 1899 and left £250,000 and under his will my father Edward Greg and his sons Thomas and Ernest benefited very considerably". Shades of great uncle Thomas of

Coles, who had also used his patrimony to shore up the wealth and standing of his brother and nephews.

Alexander, called "black Alec" within the family for his swarthy complexion, was the son with whom Edward had the best rapport. His description of his father as "a singularly loveable man and of a very simple nature, with a keen sense of humour" reveals an appealing side to his character. Both Ernest and Alexander shared their father's enthusiasm for part-time soldiering, joining the local territorial unit in which he had served. But Alec also supported his father as partner in Quarry Bank, while the other five, doubtless all too aware that it could not support them all, sought their fortunes elsewhere.

Of Edward's six sons, four had successful careers. Thomas graduated from Oxford, practised as a solicitor and inherited his uncle's estate at Coles in 1906. Edward graduated as an engineer in London and rose to be Managing Director of the Manchester firm Nasmyth Wilson Ltd. Ernest went into the sewing cotton business of James Chadwick, following in his uncle's footsteps as chairman. One might call this some payback on their expensive education, though that of course had been driven by social convention rather than any perception of a return on investment.

The most distinguished son was Robert, who passed the stiff exams for the Foreign Office. He was for some time secretary to Lord Kitchener, and was knighted for his services in 1929. He served as Ambassador at the Court of King Carol of Romania between the wars. From there he represented Britain on the Caisse des Dettes in Cairo, where he retired with his American-born wife to a large villa on the Nile. A keen Egyptologist, he was a Director of the Cairo Museum till his death in 1953.

Edward senior retired from business in 1900. When Alec's territorial unit was mobilised for the Boer war, Quarry Bank was left in the hands of a manager. Alec does not seem to have been involved in actual combat.

The subsequent Edwardian period saw a revival in the world economy, bringing better fortunes to the textile business. A wave of new mill construction began in Lancashire and west Yorkshire. Under Alec's management Quarry Bank, now a weaving-only mill, shared in this prosperity to some extent. It was helped by the timely replacement of the old 1820s water wheel, and from 1908 by investment in the new Northrop automatic loom which raised the weaver's productivity by automatic replacement of weft in the shuttle. The Northrop loom was not universally successful in Lancashire. Its introduction was resisted by the unions because of the threat higher productivity posed to the weavers' employment. In 1906 and again in 1908 its introduction at Ashton Bros caused notorious strikes, which slowed its adoption elsewhere. But the Northrop was technically well suited to the coarser cloths woven at Quarry Bank, while the enhanced productivity caused fewer problems at Styal where labour was scarce and unions had little influence.

Ernest Greg married Marian Cross, who bore him three sons and two daughters. He was the only one of the six brothers who managed to produce male heirs.

With the military experience and commitment of Ernest and Alexander, the Norcliffe Gregs shared to the full the patriotic surge that greeted the outbreak of war in 1914. Alexander and Ernest were both mobilised with their territorial units, though they were too old to be posted to the front. Instead Ernest was appointed to recruiting for the army in Wales and Cheshire. In 1917 his work was recognised by a CBE.

Daughters Madge and Helen volunteered to serve at the front as nurses and the two older sons both volunteered for the army. Arthur was twice wounded at the front before losing his life with the Royal Flying Corps. The younger Robert was killed just months before the Armistice. The family was desolated by these bereavements, but their grief was shared by many families in Styal, including employees and tenants, helping to cement the bonds within a small community.

The mill only limped through the war. After an all-too-brief post-war revival, it lapsed into further losses. In 1923 it was made into a private company, with Alexander and Ernest as prime shareholders. Alexander then withdrew, leaving Styal to take up dairy farming in Hampshire; and later retired to Westmill.

Ernest was still heavily committed to the sewing cotton business in Bolton, but on his brother's retirement he took control at Quarry Bank, delegating its management to a long-standing employee, accountant Sam Henshall. There were still nearly 200 workers, many of them his tenants, and he felt an obligation to keep the mill going for their sake. To his great credit he shouldered persistent trading losses to keep them in work.

Marian Greg died in 1931 and Ernest followed in 1934, leaving an estate valued at £340,000. It proved a watershed for the mill and the Styal community as his shares and property passed to his one surviving son, another Alexander who had been too young for war service.

Of Ernest's daughters, Madge qualified as a doctor and later married John Morley, an eminent surgeon. Helen married Guy Lloyd, who joined his father-in-law at Chadwicks. After its acquisition by the Glasgow-based firm of J & P Coats, Helen and Guy moved to Scotland, where in 1940 Guy was elected as Scottish Unionist MP for East Renfrewshire. On his retirement in 1959 he was awarded a baronetcy. The couple had four daughters and a son.

From Edward Hyde Greg's large family of six sons, young Alec would be the only surviving grandson in the male line and would have no natural children himself, though he and his wife adopted her niece and nephew. He chose to leave Styal to take up fruit farming near Northwich. Norcliffe Hall was let and subsequently sold in the 1940's.

By this time neither the mill nor the cottage properties on the estate were assets in terms of yielding any return above the costs of their upkeep. Alec therefore took the decision to donate the bulk of the estate to the National Trust, a gift completed in 1939. In the 1960s he went on to sell Quarry Bank House, garden and woodland to the Trust as well, severing his branch of the family's connections with Styal.

However Henry Philips' son, Henry Gair Greg, and his mother remained at Lode Hill and his sister, Katherine Jacks, and her family continued to live in the village, where they played a large role in supporting the Unitarian witness at Norcliffe Chapel.

An industry leader in the twilight years

The Albert Mill in Reddish enjoyed none of Quarry Bank's scenic attractions, but from the economic point of view it was a better location than rural Styal. The original mill dated from the 1840s, a workaday spinning and doubling mill, producing single and doubled yarns for sale. It had benefited from the 19th-century advances in steam generation technology and from access from the coalfields. This helped it to survive the testing times of the late Victorian era.

Henry Russell Greg, named partly to reflect his father's admiration for Lord John Russell, the Whig statesman and prime minister, proved a safer pair of hands as a mill owner than his extravagant brother Edward. But the contrast between the two sides of the family should not be exaggerated. Henry followed much the same conventional mores, sending his son to Rugby and on to Trinity College, Cambridge. Like Edward he inherited a large part of the Styal estate from his father and his son would inherit a substantial share of his uncle Arthur's estate, including further land at Styal and Reddish.

Relations between Edward's family at Norcliffe and Henry's at Lode Hill, a mock Tudor mansion built by their father in the 1860s half a mile away, were close and cordial. There was much reciprocal entertaining, with shooting parties organised on their extensive estates. With their coats of arms and large households supported by domestic servants, gardeners and gamekeepers, Robert Hyde Greg's descendants were Edwardian grandees and pillars of society. They had come a long way since the days when Samuel Greg, the only Irishman in Manchester and suspected of harbouring an Irish Republican sister, had gone in fear of a knock on the door.

In 1862 Henry Russell Greg married Emily, daughter of Samuel Stillman Gair, a Unitarian from Liverpool and sister of his older brother Robert's wife, Louisa. There was one contrast with the Norcliffe Gregs who had substantially abandoned their family's Unitarian allegiance: Unitarianism remained a dominant force in Henry's life. He endowed the new Unitarian theological college at Oxford, the former Warrington Academy, renamed Manchester College, becoming its first President.

Henry had five daughters and one son, but that son, Henry Philips Greg, exhibited something of the vision and drive of his great grandfather Samuel. When he joined his father as partner in R Greg & Co in 1887, the industry was already past its heyday. But by the time his father died in 1894 he had a thorough grasp of the business. He was especially alert to new technology and the need, in an age when indigenous spinning capacity was growing in so many of Britain's traditional markets, for specialisation and the capture of niche markets.

Henry took as his partner Alec Dowson, a relative descended from Samuel Greg junior. As the economy recovered in the new century, they replaced mules with ring spinning frames, built a large extension in 1907 and developed specialised fancy yarns for the burgeoning markets in furnishings.

Doubling was a widely-used process involving twisting together two or more single yarns to produce a stronger thread for heavy duty warps. But in fancy doubling the single yarns, which might be spun from other fibres than cotton such as, linen, wool or synthetic fibres, were fed to the spindle at different speeds. The object was not to increase tensile strength but rather to achieve a variety of decorative effects which could be specified by the customer.

In 1913 fancy doubling capacity was further extended and R Greg & Co became a lead supplier of fancy yarns for furnishings and subsequently knitwear.

The company pursued enlightened employment policies, providing a playing field, a recreation room and a club, the Albert, for its workers. In 1915 it became the first mill to appoint employee welfare officer. In 1919 it was made a private limited company. The 20th century would prove a difficult time for the industry, but this foresight would keep Albert Mill going for a further sixty years.

The Edwardian period saw renewed expansion in Britain's textile industries, along with growing wealth for Manchester, which, despite considerable diversification, still owed much of its prosperity to cotton. In Henry Philips Greg the family regained something of its former pre-eminence in the industry, albeit during its twilight years. He became an avid proponent of research and innovation, and was able to persuade and enthuse others in the industry, so that his counsel was much sought after. He gained directorships in several public joint stock companies.

In particular, as Chairman of the British Northrop Loom Company of Blackburn, Henry pioneered the introduction of automatic looms into Britain, and as Chairman of Ashton Bros he spearheaded its investment in the looms. He also played a part in their successful adoption by his cousin, Alex Greg, at Quarry Bank.

In 1917, when Lloyd George's government began to concern itself with industrial issues, it was to Henry they turned to help set up a research foundation for the cotton industry. He played a key role in the start-up in 1920 of the Shirley Institute of the British Cotton Industry Research Association, and chaired it for some years. He was also closely involved in establishing the Textile Institute and in obtaining its charter.

In 1896 Henry Philips Greg married Jenny Dibblee, a cultured lady who had studied painting in Italy. They had one son, Henry, and four daughters Emily, Barbara, Maud and Katharine. He shared his wife's interest in art; among his many honorary appointments in Manchester, he was Treasurer of the Whitworth Art Gallery and on the Committee for the City Art Gallery. He was also at various times on the Senate of

Manchester University, the Committee of the College of Technology and a Cheshire JP. A convinced Unitarian, he followed in his father's footsteps as Treasurer of Manchester College at Oxford and was a close friend of its first Master, Dr Laurence Persal Jacks, for many years editor of the Hibbert Journal and the leading Unitarian writer and preacher of his generation. The Jacks connection was reinforced by two marriages between Jacks sons and Greg daughters.

As landlord of much of Styal, Henry Philips Greg shared his cousin Ernest's concern for the welfare of his tenants and took pains to maintain and improve their properties. Like previous Gregs, he worried about alcohol abuse as landlord of Styal's Ship Inn. In 1900 he confronted the problem by founding a Village Club, endowed with premises where he could control alcohol consumption. This became the centre of community activity in the village.

Henry took great pride in his land and properties at Styal, so the compulsory purchase of a portion of his estate by Manchester Corporation for an airport came as a personal blow. This, along with demanding business and other commitments, may have hastened his death in 1936. However his estate and business, unlike that of his Norcliffe cousin, was still viable. His son Henry Gair Greg took up his father's role, both as Managing Director of R Greg & Co and paternalist landlord of half the village of Styal.

Norcliffe Hall, redeveloped into apartments, survives to this day, but the Second World War saw Lode Hill commandeered by the government. It was never restored to its former glory and was demolished in 1959. In an age of capital taxation and post war migration of the adult population to better rewarded occupations than domestic service, the grandee status of the Gregs and other families like them became a part of history.

Pressure to meet wartime needs however revived the cotton industry, and activity at the Albert Mill was stepped up. The revival continued in the immediate post-war period, when so many basic materials remained in short supply. There was further modernisation, including the replacement of steam power by electric motors. But by the mid-1950s this impetus was waning, and the solid foundations laid down by Henry Philips Greg and Alec Dowson were proving insufficient. Fancy yarns were broadly profitable, owing much to the vision of son-in-law Stopford Jacks, who joined the firm between the wars. However the plain spinning and doubling which absorbed most of the capital spend and maintenance produced a poor quality product relative to the raw cotton input. At the same time the downstream cloth markets for coarse yarns in furnishings and carpets were being steadily eroded by low-cost imports.

During the 1960s losses accumulated to the point where the mill was sold to the group which later became Coats Patons, now Coats plc. Today Quarry Bank still stands as a monument to Britain's early industrial pre-eminence, but Albert Mill was demolished in 1967 to make way for housing. So ended two and a half centuries of Greg prominence in commercial and industrial enterprise, a period that broadly coincided with the rise and decline in Britain's status as a world power.

Wealth dispersal

Through the generations the Gregs experienced a remarkably high incidence of childless marriages, a factor which sustained important recyclings of wealth. In the 20th century, however, the laws around entailed property changed, and that family tradition was broken.

When Edward Hyde Greg waived his title to the entailed property at Westmill on the death of his childless older brother, the Coles estate and properties fell to his oldest son, Thomas Tylston Greg. A gentle and learned man who followed Liberal politics, he unsuccessfully contested the Hitchen Division of Hertfordshire in successive elections. He married late in life and had no children. Shortly before his death in 1920 he was persuaded by his wife, Mary, to leave everything to her in absolute ownership.

She then quickly abandoned Westmill for London's West End, and in 1925 Coles Park and its contents were auctioned off. Greg relatives were reduced to bidding against members of the public for treasures collected by their forebears. Three years later, the house was destroyed by fire.

The site has now been redeveloped for upmarket private dwellings, but the park remains largely unchanged. Mary Greg did establish a trust in memory of her husband, which she endowed with land and properties in Westmill for the benefit of the village, thus maintaining the benevolent family tradition. However from the mid 1930s her interest switched to the Guild of St George, a charitable trust set up in the previous century by John Ruskin to promote his aesthetic and social ideals. She gave various artefacts to the Guild in her lifetime and left the residue of her estate to it upon her death, aged 99, in 1949.

In Cheshire the demise of the Albert Mill was followed in the late 20th century by a disastrous loss of landed wealth at Reddish. Henry Phillips Greg, like his grandfather, aimed to provide the security of rent income to his descendants. However, being used to stable money values after a century of stable prices, he was happy to follow the practice conventional in the northwest of leasing land to developers on chief rents fixed in perpetuity. His son, Henry, together with fellow trustee Mary Greg, who had inherited a portion of the estate from her late husband, continued the practice into the 1950s.

By the end of the century these leases had proved a financial disaster. The capital value of fixed rent streams, decimated in real terms by the savage inflation of the 1970s, had become derisory. Much of the income, divided between multiple householders and yielding only a few old shillings per annum, was effectively irrecoverable.

The Greg mausoleum in the graveyard at Knockbreda

Quarry Bank Mill

Albert Mill in the 1950s (woodcut by Barbara Greg)

Quarry Bank House today

Apprentice house at Quarry Bank

Workers' cottages at Styal

Chapter 11

Henry Gair Greg remained a substantial landowner at Styal until the 1970s. However, when he died in 1978 his will gave his tenants the option to buy the properties they occupied at probate value. This included not just cottages but several farms, along with the Ship Inn itself. Most of the tenants readily seized this opportunity, leaving only a small residue still in the family's ownership. Henry's will also provided for the sale of one family treasure, a large oil painting by Wright of Derby, at reduced heritage value to the City of Derby.

The Greg heritage

Family memorials

The Greg family has many conventional memorials in family vaults, along with memorial tablets in churches and chapels in England. They include St Bartholomew's in Wilmslow, St Mary's at Westmill, Unitarian chapels at Norcliffe and Dean Row in Cheshire and elsewhere.

The most ostentatious is the mausoleum in the graveyard at the Parish Church of Knockbreda in Belfast, commemorating Thomas and Elizabeth Greg of that city and their immediate descendants. Its large scale and baroque ornamentation testify to the wealth and standing of the 18th century Irish Gregs.

The graveyard now has many such mausolea and memorial structures to local magnates and benefactors, though not many are as large as the Gregs'. The ravages of time and the elements have taken their toll, and many are in a state of disrepair. However the Greg mausoleum was one of two restored in 2009 following several years of planning and Herculean fundraising by the Follies Trust, set up, in the words of its energetic chairman, Primrose Wilson, to "encourage the appreciation and conservation of Irish follies". Next on their programme is the neighbouring Cunningham-Douglas mausoleum, commemorating Thomas Greg's slightly notorious partner, Waddell Cunningham.

Museum of early factory life

The outstanding remaining piece of Greg heritage is the now-preserved fabric of Quarry Bank Mill at Styal together with cottages built by Samuel and Robert Hyde Greg for their employees, owned since 1939. It is worth tracing the route by which Quarry Bank reached its present status as a museum and estate open to the public. The acquisition made little difference to the mill at first. During the Second World War, under Sam Henshall, who successfully modified looms to make laundry bags, Robert Greg & Co operated as tenant of the National Trust. In the 1950s the mill was let to various other tenants for various activities, but by the 1960s it was threatened with dereliction.

Disaster was averted by heavy investment in repairs by the Trust, which raised funds by selling Quarry Bank House and its large garden and woodland to Eric Lowcock and his wife. Then in 1975 a charitable trust was formed to raise funds for the mill's development as a museum for the cotton industry open to the public. In 1984, 200 years after the mill first started up, Quarry Bank was named Museum of the Year, a prestigious national award.

Another benefit from Alec Greg's gift has been the National Trust's work on the preservation and skilful refurbishment of the cottages built by Samuel and Robert Hyde Greg for their workers. Now modernised, they provide accommodation for today's residents while preserving the character of these terraces of period dwellings. In Styal the NT has successfully preserved the fabric not just of an early cotton mill but of an early industrial community.

Posterity is indebted to those who worked for the former Museum Trust, particularly to David Sekers, its first Director, and subsequently to Josselyn Hill; and to Eric Lowcock, who toiled manfully over some forty years to maintain its eight acres of scenic garden and wooded hillsides in reasonable order.

In 2004 renewed financial pressures led to the National Trust taking direct control of the museum and in 2006 it purchased the house and garden, consolidating the whole site into a major attraction both for its heritage value and spectacular setting in the Bollin valley. Quarry Bank

House has been refurbished and a five-year plan launched to restore the gardens to Robert Hyde Greg's original design and planting. As funding is a severe constraint and the precipitous terrain of the Bollin gorge prohibits use of heavy plant, the work is very dependent on volunteer labour. Fortunately, enthusiasts from surrounding neighbourhoods willingly give their time and energy.

While the refurbished house is let to generate income, the garden was ceremonially opened to the public on March 11 2008 by Mrs Katharine Gore, née Jacks, a descendant of Samuel Greg brought up in Styal. Its heritage significance was further recognised on May 7 2008 by an official visit by HRH The Princess Royal.

A proud legacy

The Gregs take their place alongside many families who spearheaded the first industrial revolution. In the early days they exemplified the merchants and risk takers, men with the imagination and drive to exploit trading opportunities and invest in new technology. The family will inevitably be remembered primarily for their role in the early cotton industry, of which Quarry Bank is a fitting memento.

We must not forget the Gregs' involvement in smuggling and slave ownership - the first perhaps pardonable in the context of the times; the second less so. But family members made positive contributions in other fields - financial services, agriculture, horticulture, politics, art, literature, diplomacy, community and other endowments.

Overall, it is a history in which their descendants can take pride.

GREG FAMILY TREES

Robert Hyde of Norcliffe m Mary Philips in 1824
1795-1875   1799-????

Robert Philips	Edward Hyde	Caroline	Hannah Sophia	Henry Russell	Arthur
1826-1906	1827-1910	1828-1865	1831-1914	1834-1894	1835-1899
m Louisa Gair	m Margaret Broadbent		m Benson Rathbone	m Emily Gair	m Margaret Leister

Sons of Robert Hyde of Norcliffe

(1) Edward Hyde m Margaret Broadbent in 1856
1827-1910

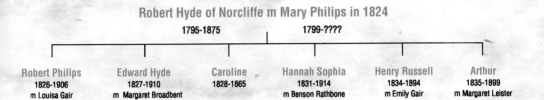

Thos Tylston	Ernest W'm	Edw'd Hyde	Robert Alexander	John Tylston	R'bt Hyde
1868-1920	1862-1934	???	1867-1953	???	??-1953
m Mary Hope no issue	m Marian Cross		married no issue	married, 2 daughters	married no issue

Edward Hyde also had 3 daughters, Caroline, who died in infancy, Margaret and Beatrice, about whom nothing has come down.

(2) Henry Russell m Emily Gair in 1860
1834-1894

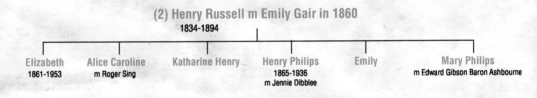

Elizabeth	Alice Caroline	Katharine Henry	Henry Philips	Emily	Mary Philips
1861-1953	m Roger Sing		1865-1936		m Edward Gibson Baron Ashbourne
			m Jennie Dibblee		

Son of Edward Hyde

Ernest William m Marian Cross 1888
1862-1934

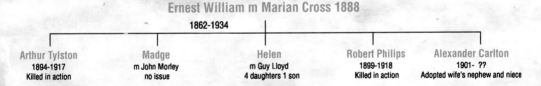

Arthur Tylston	Madge	Helen	Robert Philips	Alexander Carlton
1894-1917	m John Morley	m Guy Lloyd	1899-1918	1901- ??
Killed in action	no issue	4 daughters 1 son	Killed in action	Adopted wife's nephew and niece

Son of Henry Russell

Henry Philips m Jennie Dibblee
1865-1936

Emily Russell	Barbara	Henry Gair	Maud Philips	Katharine Hyde
1896-1965	1900-1983	1902-1978	1903-1964	1905-1999
m Maurice Jacks	m Norman Janes		m John Tremayne	m Stopford Jacks
No issue	2 daughters 1 son		3 sons	2 daughters

111

GREG FAMILY TREES

James of Ochiltree
|
John of Ochiltree and Belfast m Jane
1693-1783

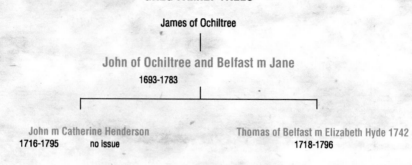

John m Catherine Henderson	Thomas of Belfast m Elizabeth Hyde 1742
1716-1795 no issue	1718-1796

Thomas of Belfast m Elizabeth Hyde 1742
1718-1796

John	Mary	Jane	Thomas	Sarah	Samuel	Eleanor	Cunningham	Margaret
1746-1780	1748-??	1750-1813	1752-1832	1755-??	1758-1834	1759-1847	1761-???	1764-1793
			m Margaret Hibbert	m Lyle	m Hannah Lightbody	m Warre	m Gason	m Batt

A further 5 of Thomas of Belfast's children died in infancy

Sons of Thomas of Belfast

(1) Thomas of Coles m Margaret Hibbert 1778
1752-1832   1750-1808
No Issue

(2) Samuel of Quarry Bank m Hannah Lightbody 1789
1758-1834   1766-1828

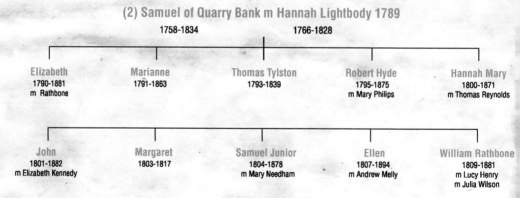

Elizabeth	Marianne	Thomas Tylston	Robert Hyde	Hannah Mary
1790-1881	1791-1863	1793-1839	1795-1875	1800-1871
m Rathbone			m Mary Philips	m Thomas Reynolds

John	Margaret	Samuel Junior	Ellen	William Rathbone
1801-1882	1803-1817	1804-1878	1807-1894	1809-1881
m Elizabeth Kennedy		m Mary Needham	m Andrew Melly	m Lucy Henry
				m Julia Wilson

3 of Samuel's children died in infancy

112